CW00693946

# Multi-Ethnic Britain

## Nance Lui Fyson

Batsford Academic and Educational Ltd    London

# Contents

© Nance Lui Fyson 1984
First published 1984

All rights reserved. No part of this publication may be reproduced, in any form or by any means, without permission from the Publisher

Typeset by Tek-Art Ltd, Kent
and printed in Great Britain by
R.J. Acford
Chichester, Sussex
for the publishers
Batsford Academic and Educational Ltd,
an imprint of B.T. Batsford Ltd,
4 Fitzhardinge Street
London W1H 0AH

ISBN 0 7134 3657 3

ACKNOWLEDGMENT

The Author and Publishers thank the following for their kind permission to use copyright illustrations in this book: Birmingham Post & Mail, page 46; Simon Clark, page 65; Express Newspapers Ltd, pages 23, 59, 61, 64; Alison Foster, pages 37, 54; Richard and Sally Greenhill, pages 4, 7 (top), 10, 12, 15, 18, 19, 20, 22, 29, 30, 32, 41, 42, 45, 51, 53, 56, 68 (right); The Guardian, pages 6, 14, 17, 44, 49, 52, 63, 67; John and Penny Hubley, pages 11, 25, 27, 28, 68 (left); ILEA Learning Materials Service, page 39; Neil Libbert, page 3; The Observer, pages 7 (bottom), 60; Open University Photos Department, page 50; Times Newspapers Ltd, pages 16, 35, 47. The diagrams on pages 8, 9 and 29 were drawn by R.F. Brien.

"We must learn to live together as brothers, or perish together as fools."
Martin Luther King (Black American civil rights leader)

52230

RLL/FYS
Resources section

# The Melting Pot

Are you "British", *truly* British? If so, you're from a very mixed background indeed. There have been waves of settlers intermarrying in Britain for thousands of years. Immigrants came from continental Europe long before the birth of Christ.

The first detailed records we have of foreigners coming to the country are from the Roman conquest in the first century AD. The land that is now called England and Wales was part of the Roman Empire for four hundred years.

After the Roman armies left Britain, other settlers came in much larger numbers. These Angles, Saxons, Frisians and Jutes came over the North Sea in the fifth and sixth centuries. It was the Angles (from what is now Denmark) who gave the name to England (Angleland).

In the ninth and tenth centuries there were more immigrants from the far north of Europe. These were the Vikings who came at first to plunder and later to settle as farmers.

During the Norman Conquest of 1066 William the Conqueror came from northern France with many soldiers and noble families. These immigrants stayed and intermarried with those already here. Britain was at that time already a great mix of peoples.

African slaves were brought to work in England from about the year 1550. There were thousands in the country by the eighteenth century. In 1772 slavery was made illegal. Many ex-slaves gradually intermarried and became part of "the British".

Some groups began arriving as refugees. New Protestant religious groups began in Holland, France and Germany. They came to England to escape persecution by the Roman Catholic Church. (Henry VIII had changed England's official religion to Protestant in the 1530s.) Thousands of Dutch Protestants came in 1567, followed by Huguenots from France in about 1660. Nearly 100,000 Huguenots had come by 1700. These immigrants brought skills such as weaving and lace-making, and were welcomed by "the English".

Jews also sought refuge in England. There were Jewish communities in many towns by the year 1200. Christians forbade them to follow

Arabs on the streets of London. Hundreds of thousands of foreigners from many countries visit Britain each year, spending millions of pounds. There are also permanent communities of foreigners. Thousands from the Middle East live here – but keep their links back home.

certain trades, own land or carry arms. There were hostilities against the Jews and in 1290 about 16,000 were expelled. Jewish immigration was allowed again from the mid-sixteenth century. By the early eighteenth century thousands of Jews had come from Spain and Portugal, escaping persecution in the Inquisition. Later in the eighteenth century Jews began to arrive from Poland and Germany. Jews coming in the 1890s were from Lithuania and Russia, escaping from the campaigns of terror (called "pogroms") against them. Another wave of Jewish refugees came in the 1930s, escaping the persecution of Hitler's Germany.

Irish immigrants to mainland Britain have been the largest group of foreigners to settle. Since the 1750s thousands have come looking for work and a better life. Many were "navvies", building canals in the years 1760 to 1820. In the mid-nineteenth century the potato blight led to food shortages, causing even more Irish to leave their country. Many came to cities such as Liverpool, Manchester and London. Being poor, the Irish immigrants lived in overcrowded slums. Some English looked down on them. These Irish suffered in the way that recent black immigrants are sometimes suffering abuse. The "British", themselves a product of much multi-ethnic mixing over the centuries, have not always been kind to people easily recognizable as recent "foreigners".

Britain's former Empire is now nearly all independent states. Most have kept a link with Britain as part of the Commonwealth of nations. "Old Commonwealth" nations are those that were given full independence by 1931. These included the former dominions of Canada, Australia, New Zealand and South Africa which had many white European settlers. (South Africa is no longer in the Commonwealth and so is no longer grouped with the "Old Commonwealth".) The colonies in Asia, the West Indies, and Africa were not given independence until after the Second World War. These became known as "New Commonwealth" countries.

## ENCOURAGING PEOPLE TO COME

Britain passed a British Nationality Act in 1948. It declared Commonwealth citizens "citizens of the United Kingdom and Colonies". As British passport holders, these people had the right to come to Britain to live.

Britain actually had a *shortage* of workers in semi-skilled jobs after the Second World War. Britain *encouraged* immigrants to come. Buildings were needed because of bomb damage and lack of construction during the war. The new National Health Service needed workers as well. Factories were turning out all the goods that people had missed in wartime. More labour was needed. A government department set up to recruit foreign workers brought over 350,000 Europeans between the years 1945 and 1957.

London Transport opened a recruiting office in Barbados in 1956. The National Health Service and the Hotels and Restaurants Association followed this lead. These drives were quite successful. While about 9,000 West Indians came in 1954, the number was nearly 30,000 in 1956.

The immigration of black people from Asia, Africa and Latin America was not large, but it began to worry some people in Britain. In 1960 the automatic right of free entry for New Commonwealth citizens was taken away. The first Commonwealth Immigration Act was passed which applied to *New* Commonwealth citizens only. Black immigrants were being considered quite differently from whites. Entry into Britain from the New Commonwealth was to be on the basis of work vouchers. Parliament each year decided on the number of vouchers to be granted.

Many immigrants had planned to come to Britain, work, save some money and then return home. Many decided instead to stay, as jobs were so much harder to find in their own countries. They began bringing over their wives and children under age sixteen. These "dependants" did not need work vouchers.

In 1968 the second Commonwealth Immigration Act was passed. This kept the right of free entry only for those British passport holders whose fathers or grandfathers had been born in the UK. These people are called "patrials". This Act was also criticized by some for treating blacks differently from whites. (Whites are much more likely than blacks to be "patrials".)

Another Commonwealth Immigration Act came into operation on 1 January 1973. This said that work permits allowing entry into Britain would be issued only for jobs requiring

◄Businessman Ajit Singh Rai came to Britain from India in 1956. He has a university degree and expected to find a job according to his qualifications: "But if I could get a job at all it was a night job and the dirtiest job. The whole lot of us that came to this country in the 1950s had to live with the very crudest type of racial discrimination. We were offered only the lowest-paid jobs. We are still facing racial discrimination now in almost all forms of life. The difference now is that the ethnic minorities have started asserting themselves." A.S. Rai has been active in the Indian Workers Association (IWA). This provides help and services to the Indian community and pressures the government on behalf of ethnic minorities.

particular professional qualifications, skill or experience. These restrictions were for *anyone* outside the EEC wanting to work and live in Britain. "Patrials" did still keep their right to free entry. Every other Commonwealth and non-EEC citizen would need a work permit or permission to enter. Parliament would control the numbers to be allowed in.

Laws regarding immigration and nationality are still being added. A new British Nationality Act came into force at the start of 1983. Citizens of the UK and Colonies who have the right of abode in the UK now automatically have British citizenship. One of the biggest changes made by the new Act is that a child born in the UK is now no longer automatically a British citizen. He or she is only a citizen if at the time of birth the father or mother is a British citizen or "settled in the UK" (meaning there is no time limit on how long they may remain).

Most people do not realize how strictly immigration is now controlled. Since 1973 only three categories of people from the Commonwealth other than patrials have been allowed to settle in Britain:
(1) those with special skills in short supply here;
(2) close dependants of people already lawfully settled here;
(3) holders of UK passports who have been driven out of the countries in which they have been living and who have no other citizenship.

Most people also do not realize that more people are now *leaving* Britain than coming here to live. In 1982 177,000 people came to live in the UK – but 80,000 *more* (257,000) emigrated to other countries. The Southeast of England is the area most affected, both by people leaving and by people coming in.

By far the largest number of immigrants to Britain in 1982 were from EEC countries. The level of immigration from the New Commonwealth and Pakistan was at its lowest since controls were first imposed in 1962. Migration between Britain and the Caribbean actually went into *reverse*. More people left Britain to live there than the other way round.

Only about 2,000 people from the Caribbean came to settle in Britain.

Britain certainly isn't the only country to have immigrants from other countries. Migration from country to country and continent to continent has been a world pattern since man first appeared. Over 15 million immigrants now living in Western Europe have come from a wide range of countries. Britons themselves have emigrated to Australia, Canada, the USA, Africa, Asia . . . . Those Britons who have left have often hoped for a better job and higher standard of living. This was also the reason why many people came to Britain from the New Commonwealth and Pakistan.

## THE PROMISED LAND?

"It may be that blacks are in the same boat as poor whites; but we are on different decks." This remark (by youth worker Tony Ottey in 1977) was supported in an early 1982 Government White Paper on racial disadvantage. It agreed that Britain's black ethnic minorities live "to a disproportionate extent" in decaying urban areas with the worst housing and the highest unemployment.

A Parliamentary Home Affairs Committee report on *Racial Disadvantage* was published in 1981. This made over 50 recommendations to try to improve the disadvantages faced by ethnic minorities. The Scarman Report was produced after riots in several British cities in 1981. This report also called for more action: "Given the special problems of the ethnic minorities . . . justice requires that special programmes should be adopted . . .".

The minorities themselves are speaking up more. In 1980 a "Visible Minority Survey Report" talked to 114 leaders and 800 representatives of the black communities. Their view of life in Britain in the 1980s showed a "mood of frustration, grievance and fears for the future".

This book looks at just some of the background of Britain's ethnic minority

▲

Mrs Aruna Bhatia is one woman affected by the 1983 change in immigration rules on foreign husbands. She lives in Britain but married an Asian in Kenya in 1982. Mrs Bhatia is a British citizen who came to the UK from Tanzania in 1967. Until the 1983 change, Mrs Bhatia was not allowed to bring her foreign husband to the UK (though if a man, could have brought in a wife). The new rule still excludes the foreign husbands of women living in the UK who are not British citizens. (The old rule admitted foreign husbands if the woman had been born in Britain or had a parent born here – which helped mostly whites. There was much clamour that the old rule was "racist" and "sexist".) The difficulty with immigration laws is to be fair to individuals – and yet keep overall control over numbers.

communities. The focus is on minorities from the New Commonwealth countries and Pakistan. These communities are facing some special difficulties. But minorities should not be thought of as "problems". Ethnic minorities have made and are making valuable contributions to life in Britain. As a 1977 Government Green Paper said: "Immigrant families offer an enrichment of our culture . . . if only we have the imagination to accept it."

Some ethnic minority problems are due to a lack of understanding and lack of full acceptance by the majority. The Head of the Commission for Racial Equality put it bluntly: "It is not the minority communities that are 'the problem'. The real 'problem' is with the white community."

The Ly family are Vietnamese and among the most recent wave of refugees to the UK. In 1979 the Vietnamese government expelled ethnic Chinese from the country. Thousands of homeless "boat people" were accepted by some countries – including over 5,000 by Britain. Refugees went first to reception centres, where they were helped to learn some English. Finding homes and jobs has not been easy. Mr Ly owned a bus fleet in Hanoi. His wife and daughters are seamstresses. Two sons have begun work in a factory here, and one works at carpentry. Some of the refugees have been professionals – doctors, dentists, engineers. ▼

The Italian Hospital in London offers a wide range of medical treatment for the capital's 100,000 Italians. It is supported solely by charity. There are Italian pictures on the walls, Italian magazines in the waiting room, and Italian nuns on the staff. Signs are in Italian as well as English. The daily menu has mainly pasta meals. "Some Italian patients are frightened to go to a NHS hospital because they fear they may not be understood by the staff."

# How Many? ... From Where?

How many ethnic minority people are there in Britain? From which countries have they come?

## THE CENSUS

A main source of figures is the Census. This national survey is taken every ten years and shows statistics about age, household-structure, location, housing, employment, and educational qualifications of the whole population. Separate groups within this can be identified. The Census does not collect information directly about "race", but there is data on where people were born, and their parents' birthplaces.

Information about "birthplaces" can give a misleading idea about people's race. Many white people were born in the New Commonwealth while their parents were working overseas. Similarly, the children of many non-white New Commonwealth immigrants have been born in Britain. To have a more accurate picture about ethnic minorities, it was proposed that people should indicate their "racial or ethnic group" for the 1981 census. This was the subject of hot debate and finally dropped.

## "FOREIGN-BORN"

The 1981 census showed that over 3½ million people living in Britain were born overseas. This formed nearly 7% of the total population. (The figures do include a number of British people who were born abroad, such as children of diplomatic staff. The figures do *not* include children born in this country to people who were born overseas.)

The circle chart shows the main areas in which the 3½ million "foreigners" in Britain were born. About 43% of these were born in New Commonwealth countries and Pakistan. (Old Commonwealth countries include Australia, Canada and New Zealand.) (Source: Country of Birth Tables, 1981 Census)

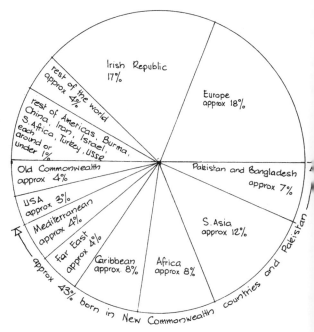

Britain is hardly swamped by foreigners – or blacks! Of the total UK population, *the less than 7% foreign-born* could be shown like this:

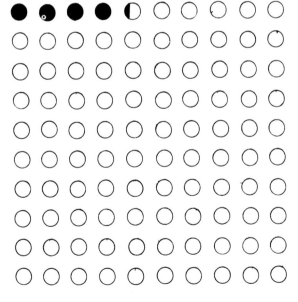

△ = foreign-born

Of the total UK population, *the total number of "non-whites" (including those born in the UK)* could be shown like this:

● = non-whites usually resident in UK

The Office of Population Census and Surveys announced figures in 1983 saying that there were about 2.2 million "non-whites" living in Britain (approximately 4.1% of the total UK population). *Over 40% of these "non-whites" were actually born in Britain.* New Commonwealth and Pakistani immigrants have tended to settle in some parts of Britain more than others (mainly because of jobs). Nearly 80% of the "non-white" population is concentrated in 10% of census enumeration districts. The main areas where non-white ethnic minorities live and work are London, Birmingham, Leicester, Bradford and Manchester. Overall, nearly 60% of African, West Indian, Indian and Pakistani and Bangladeshi immigrants have settled in the Southeast of England. Depending on where in Britain YOU live, you may be much more or less likely to meet and know people from non-white ethnic minority groups.

Here are some very brief introductions to the main New Commonwealth and Pakistani immigrant groups living in Britain.

## WEST INDIANS

West Indians in Britain have come mainly from a few English-speaking islands in the Caribbean. About 60% are from Jamaica, which was taken over by the British in 1670 until independence in 1962. First of the post-Second World War black immigrants were the nearly 500 men from Jamaica on a ship called the *Empire Windrush*. Many of these men had been stationed in the UK during the war, when they served in the Royal Air Force. Like other immigrants at this time, they were encouraged to come to fill the many jobs open.

Other West Indian immigrants are mainly from Trinidad and Tobago, Guyana, Barbados and islands such as Grenada, St Lucia, St Kitts and Nevis.

Most West Indians in Britain are of African origin. African slaves were taken forcibly by Europeans to work on the Caribbean plantations. By 1807 the trade had taken more than a quarter of a million slaves to Jamaica and tens of thousands more to other islands. Slavery was abolished in the British West Indies in 1834.

When black Africans were taken to the Caribbean as slaves, they were forced to adopt Western European culture. This included the Christian religion. The Pentecostal and Holiness churches and the Seventh-day Adventists in Britain have been showing a sharp rise in membership. These churches have a large West Indian and African following. (Meanwhile, the long-established Christian churches of Britain – Anglicans, Methodists, Roman Catholics, and Baptists – have all been losing members.)

There are also West Indians in Britain of Asian origin. In 1869 West Indian planters began recruiting workers by the "indenture" system. This meant that they offered free passage to and from the colony and a fixed wage, in exchange for working a set number of years on the plantation. About 150,000 workers from India and China came to Trinidad under this system during the late nineteenth and early twentieth centuries.

Trinidad and Tobago is now a two-island state, and Guyana is actually on the mainland of South America. These were both formerly British colonies, which became independent in 1962 and 1966. Because of the influx of slaves, indentured workers and others, these states include people of African, East Indian, Chinese and European origin. The main religions are Christianity, Hinduism and Islam. Indo-Trinidadians and Indo-Guyanese are now about half the population in Trinidad and just over

Ashton Gibson (third from the left) came to Britain from Barbados in 1952. He founded West Indian Concern Ltd in North London – one of many self-help groups formed by ethnic minorities. "It is crystal clear that we are having problems over and above other people, problems that are reflected out of all proportion to our number . . . . The West Indian is in a dreamland. He doesn't know where he is, who he is, where he is going. Slavery has really taken away his culture. The Asians have not a legacy of slavery. They have been able to bring with them a strong culture and a strong religion and ability to keep together . . . "

half the population in Guyana. A number of these East Indians came to Britain in the 1950s and '60s, to work and study.

## GUJARATIS

Gujarat state is one of the richest areas of India. There is much productive farming and the largest dairy plant in Asia. There are also other industries, especially textiles. Ahmedabad, the state capital, has been called the "Manchester of India".

Gujaratis have been coming to Britain since the late nineteenth century. They have included Mahatma Gandhi, who came as a law student. (He later led India to independence in

Gujaratis in Leeds at a Hindu prayer meeting. This is held every Friday evening in a room of the community leader's home. The shrine in the background, called *puja*, is made by the worshippers.

1947). Larger migration began after the Second World War. Gujaratis with experience in textile industries and foundries came to make up the shortage of workers here. Later, more Asians with a Gujarati background came from countries of East Africa.

Gujaratis are known as very hard-working, industrious people, with a flair for business. Today, there are at least fifty Gujarati-owned firms in the UK, that turn over yearly at least one million pounds. Most Gujaratis have not done nearly *so* well, but are familiar as small shopkeepers and newsagents in a number of towns. Over half of the 1200 sub-post offices in London are owned by Gujaratis. Not all Gujaratis are "Patels", but this is one common Gujarati name. (The word means "landowner".) There are now over seven pages of "Patels" in the London directory alone.

Most Gujaratis in Britain follow the Hindu

Sikhs at the start of a *gurdwara* (temple) service.

religion. This is the main religion of India, followed by about 80% of the people there. Most religious Hindus are vegetarian. Eating meat, especially beef, is forbidden. As with other religions, some people are much more strict than others in following the practices.

Devout Hindus believe in reincarnation (life after death). Hindu worship (Puja) takes place most often in the home. Rites are performed by the eldest member when the family is gathered together. Worship in temples is important for special occasions.

The traditional Hindu caste system separates people as they are born into higher and lower social positions. Caste is related to occupation. While people in the same caste may be either rich or poor, people may not move from one caste to another. There are four main categories, and sub-castes within these: Brahmans (priests), Kshatriyas (rulers and warriors), Vaishyas (businessmen and farmers) and Sudras (the lowest caste of labourers and untouchables).

It is now forbidden by law in India to discriminate against people because of their caste, and the barriers are breaking down. But the system does persist and can be seen within Britain's Hindu community. Social sub-groups are loyal to each other and support each other like a large, extended family.

Hindus celebrate a large number of festivals. One of the most important is *Diwali* – a festival of lights in October/November. This marks the start of the Hindu New Year. It is a time, like Christmas, for family reunions and sending cards to relatives in other parts of the world. *Diwali* also marks the start of the new Hindu business year. Annual accounts are closed and the goddess of wealth, Lakshmi, is honoured. *Holi* takes place at the beginning of spring, as a festival of colours. *Navratri* is an autumn Festival of Nine Nights leading up to a

*Dashara/Dussehra* celebration. There are processions, songs and folk dances.

## PUNJABIS

Most Punjabis in Britain are Asians who have come from the state of Punjab in north India. (There is a Pakistani Province of Punjab as well.)

The Indian Punjab is mainly a farming area, with villages. It is one of the most economically advanced parts of the country. Production in farming has increased greatly and many manufactured goods are made as well. This is the homeland of the Sikh people. Only 2% of the Indian population follow this religion. Many people living in the Punjab are not Sikhs, but most Punjabis in Britain are.

The Punjab was under British rule for nearly a hundred years. During the Second World War many Sikhs fought in the British forces. Sikhs have a tradition as proud fighters. In the 1950s and early 1960s the demand for workers in Britain prompted some Sikhs who had fought for Britain to return. Others came as well. They came to areas like the West Midlands where foundries, steel works and other industries needed labour. In the 1960s and 1970s there was further migration of Sikhs amongst the Asians coming from East Africa.

(There were already communities of Indians living in Britain before the Second World War. In the late nineteenth and earlier this century Indian seamen landed in ports such as Liverpool and Cardiff. Sometimes they stayed to work in factories. There was also a more professional community – doctors, students, businessmen.)

The word "Sikh" means literally "disciple". The earliest Sikhs were actually breaking away from the Hindu religion in the sixteenth century. Sikhism as it is today was formed largely by the tenth and last of the Sikh teachers, Guru Gobind Singh who led until 1708. He began the practice of Sikh men taking the surname "Singh", meaning "lion". Women's surnames all include "Kaur", meaning "princess".

There are five requirements in the uniform worn by devout Sikh males. One is a steel bracelet, and another is that the hair and beard should not be cut. This has led to many Sikhs wearing turbans to cover their heads. An important fact of Sikhism is that everyone is treated alike. Sikhs have never had a caste system ranking some people as "better" than others.

Most Sikhs do eat meat, but only if the animal is slaughtered in a special way, called "Halal". Every Sikh *gurdwara* or temple has a kitchen or dining area where the congregation eat together after services.

Many Sikhs are outgoing and extroverted. Self-denial is not a strong Sikh tradition. The pleasures of laughter, eating and dressing well are to be enjoyed. Sikhs are often prominent in sport. *Kabaddi* is one rough game popular in Punjabi villages. It is like rugby – without the ball.

## PAKISTANIS

Pakistan was created as a homeland for Muslims at the time of Indian independence in 1947. (Muslims are followers of a religion called Islam.) What is now called Pakistan was then West Pakistan. East Pakistan has since become the separate country of Bangladesh.

Most of Britain's Pakistani community comes from around the town of Mirpur. This is a hilly farming area which is dry for much of the year. Strictly speaking, Mirpur is not in Pakistan but in the part of Kashmir which Pakistan controls. This is called Azad or free Kashmir. Since the end of British rule, India and Pakistan have argued over control of the area. Mirpuris have faced much disturbance. Many lost their homes and had to move out. Another factor prompting migration was a hydro-electric dam, the Mangla Dam, built by the Pakistani government.

Many young Mirpuris have been going to sea since early this century. Some docked in British ports and stayed. Others served in British forces during the Second World War and then settled

A mother and son enjoy Britain's first Muslim funfair in 1982. This was set up so that Leicester's 15,000 Muslims could celebrate the end of Ramadan in the traditional way. (Funfairs are a popular part of the festivities in Islamic centres of India, Pakistan and East Africa.)

here. More came as part of the post-war need for workers in Britain.

Almost all the people from Pakistan and Bangladesh in Britain follow Islam. The Muslim Holy Book, the Koran, is thought the direct word of Allah (God). Muslims do not eat pork and many only eat other meat which is "Halal" (blessed and killed in a special way).

Strict Muslims perform five daily prayers. Before each, hands and feet are washed, the mouth and nose are rinsed, and wet hands are passed over the head. During the month of Ramadan, there is fasting from dawn to dusk. Traditionally, Muslim women should follow *purdah* by veiling or covering their heads and bodies and not mixing freely with the men.

The *Biraderi* (brotherhood or clan) is the basic social organization in much of Pakistan (as well as India and Bangladesh). This is a wide network of relatives and friends who exchange support for each other as it is needed. Many immigrants have relied on this help as they have come to Britain.

## BENGALIS

The country name "Bangladesh" means "the land of the Bengali people". This area was called East Pakistan until 1971. There are also Bengalis living in the adjoining state of West Bengal in India. Most Bengalis in Britain are from the rural area of Sylhet in Bangladesh.

Bangladesh is a land of rivers which flood the farmlands during the monsoon rains. Sylhet has one of the world's wettest climates. During the monsoon, nearly 70% of the area is not accessible by road. Boats are hand-paddled through the floodwater.

During the First World War Britain needed manpower for the British Merchant Navy. The British government opened recruiting centres in Bombay and Calcutta and many Sylhetis went to Calcutta to sign on. Recruits continued to join for decades.

In the early and mid-1950s Bengali men came

Brick Lane Mosque, East End, London. The building was once a Huguenot church, then became a Jewish synagogue – and is now a Muslim mosque for the Bengali community. The Brick Lane area has had a succession of ethnic minorities centred there over the years.

to work in the kitchens of London's hotels and clubs. Some became employed in factories. Britain needed their labour and they were encouraged to come. Bengali immigrants in the 1960s were still mainly men. As with other groups, most intended to return home, but gradually families were brought over.

Many Bengalis have established themselves as restaurant owners and workers. The estimate is that 80% of the so-called Indian and Pakistani restaurants in Britain are in fact run by people from Bangladesh. Most of these restaurants serve the northern Indian dishes which are thought to be favoured by English customers.

The largest settlement of Bengalis is in the East End of London. In the early 1970s about 2% of the total population of Tower Hamlets borough was of Sylhetic origin. By the early 1980s nearly 20% of the borough descended from that area. The growth of the community has been partly caused by families coming over. Bengalis have also moved in from other areas of Britain. Many Bengalis work in the clothing industry in and around Brick Lane.

Bengalis are regarded as fairly quiet, peace-loving people – but capable of going to the other extreme if oppressed. Most Bengalis, like Pakistanis, follow the religion of Islam.

## EAST AFRICAN ASIANS

East African Asians emigrated to Britain mainly as refugees. When Kenya became an independent country in 1963, the 115,000 Asians there were given the choice of becoming Kenyan or staying British. About 95,000 chose to keep their UK citizenship. These Asians were mainly traders and professional people. In 1967 the Kenyan government said that all non-Kenyan citizens would be treated as foreigners. (The government wanted to create more opportunities for black Africans.) By February 1968 about 44,000 Kenyan Asians had come to Britain. The Resettlement Board for Kenyans operated until 1972, to help incoming Asians find homes and jobs in Britain.

A similar event took place in Uganda in 1972. The Ugandan President declared that he was expelling all Asians with British passports. There were threats of violence. The British government quickly provided an emergency airlift to bring Ugandan Asians with British passports to the UK. Another Resettlement Board was set up for them, operating until 1974.

Many of the Asian immigrants from East Africa are from urban areas, where they worked as shopkeepers and traders. In contrast to this, most immigrants from the Indian subcontinent are from rural village areas. In some ways, this has made it easier for East African Asians to adapt to urban life in Britain. But, as refugees, the East African Asians have had other difficulties.

## CHINESE

Hong Kong is the third largest financial centre in the world (after New York and London). It is also a large manufacturing centre, with 90% of its goods being exported. Hong Kong is the world's largest exporter of garments, toys and watches. But all this takes place on Hong Kong island and Kowloon. There is a much larger area of countryside known as the "New Territories". Most Chinese in Britain today come from this rural part of Hong Kong.

In the early nineteenth century Chinese were recruited as sailors for British ships which were trading in the Far East. By the late 1860s there were Chinese living in London's dockland and

Timothy Mo was born in Hong Kong to a Chinese father and English mother. He has lived in England since he was ten and is now a struggling author. In 1982 he was short-listed for Britain's top two literary prizes. His second novel was set among the Chinese in Britain, telling the story of a waiter. Timothy Mo doesn't think the Chinese character lends itself easily to writing: "The family is first, not the individual. It's individuals who write books."

in Liverpool. Many worked in the laundry business.

There are Chinese students and nurses in Britain who have come from Singapore and Malaysia as well as Hong Kong. There are also Chinese professionals who came from these and other places as well. It was what happened in the late 1940s and '50s that prompted larger migration from Hong Kong.

The Communist victory in China in 1949 caused many Chinese to flee to the New Territories. This led to much overcrowding. Some people in the New Territories (which was British since 1898) took their entitlement to a British passport and came to the UK. Farming changes also prompted many to leave. The Chinese who came to Britain went mainly into the restaurant trade. In the late 1950s and '60s

The Northern Cyprus Folk Dance Society performed at the start of "London Entertains". This was a festival held in 1982 to help Londoners learn more about the ethnic communities living amongst them.

the number of Chinese restaurants in Britain more than doubled. There was a growing taste in Britain for Chinese food and eating out generally.

About 40% of the UK Chinese live in the Greater London area. A survey was taken in 1972 around Gerrard Street. This is Britain's largest Chinatown, in a few streets behind Piccadilly Circus. The early 1970s list showed 28 Chinese restaurants, two Chinese doctors, a Chinese accountant, 15 Chinese firms and shops and one Chinese cinema. Since 1972 this list has grown visibly, with more Chinese restaurants and supermarkets especially.

Chinese communities in Britain still keep to traditional "religions" such as Confucianism, Taoism and Buddhism. These are all based on the teachings of different philosophers.

## CYPRIOTS

Cyprus, in the Eastern Mediterranean, is

mainly an agricultural country. There are about six hundred villages across the island. Cyprus was a British Crown colony from 1925 to 1960. Most Cypriots who have come to Britain came in the 1950s, '60s and '70s, partly because of struggles for power between the Greek and Turkish communities. In 1974 the Turkish army invaded Cyprus and occupied 40% of the territory, hoping for a separate Turkish-Cypriot part of the island. Half the population of the island was uprooted, with Greek Cypriots in the North fleeing to the South and Turkish Cypriots in the South fleeing to the occupied North. Many uprooted people came to the UK at that time. Most Cypriots in Britain are Greek-Cypriots, but nearly a fifth are Turkish-Cypriots. Greek Cypriots are Christians belonging to the Orthodox Church, while Turkish Cypriots are Muslim.

## AFRICAN BLACKS

Black people directly from Africa are a long-established minority group in Britain. There were small numbers in the UK before 1600. In the seventeenth and eighteenth centuries it was fashionable for rich ladies to have black servants. By the nineteenth century larger numbers of African blacks came over to England. Seamen settled, and sons of Chiefs came for education. During the First World War more African blacks came to work in munition factories. Students and other professional and business people have come as well.

There is an Africa Centre in London which has classes for Africans and exhibitions and courses about Africa. A Calabash Restaurant serves African dishes.

Felix Cobbson came to Britain from Ghana at the age of eighteen. He trained in art and now teaches Creative Activities in a UK school – including African drumming and dancing. These are very popular with British teenagers. "Teaching the children African music was tough at the beginning because they had never heard real African music. They found a cross-rhythm a bit off-putting. Now they know that African music is not just taking the drums and banging."

# Family Life

Ethnic minorities in Britain live much the same as everyone else. However, there are some traditions from their countries of origin which are carried on in this country. These are much stronger amongst some families than others.

```
   INDIANS, PAKISTANIS, BANGLADESHIS
```

The traditional family in the Indian subcontinent is a "joint" or "extended" family. This may mean three or even four generations living together. Family ties are important, including many obligations and duties. The individual's wishes are less important than those of the family group. This joint family structure is most important in rural villages where 80% of people in the Indian subcontinent live. Less than one fifth of Asian immigrants in Britain have come from urban areas, and so the extended family tie remains fairly strong here.

On the Indian subcontinent there is no Welfare State nor national insurance to look after old and other dependent people. The joint family is a way of looking after everyone's needs. Duties and burdens are shared. Different relatives all have separate titles. The Bengali language has sixty-four different names for various relations! Old people are highly respected in traditional families, with the eldest male normally the head.

Marriage is regarded as the union of families rather than of two individuals. Daughters leave to become part of their husband's joint family. A dowry of gifts may be paid by the bride's

A.S. Rai (see page 4) and family. The parents were born in India and came to Britain in the 1950s. One child was born in India, and the other three were born in the UK. A.S. Rai: "The youth of our communities became disgruntled not only against the authorities but also against their own leadership. Many of the youth do not realize how we have struggled. Our new generation will not stand all the insults, all the deprivations, all the unfairness which we had to live with in the past. Our children who were born here lead two lives, one at their homes and another in the outside world. There must be compromise. The children who were born here should give some concession to their parents who were born in a different atmosphere. There are very deep tensions within the families. It will take some time before it all settles down."

19

parents. Dowries are no longer legal in India, but the practice carries on – amongst Asians in Britain as well.

It is the tradition for parents to arrange marriages for their children. In most cases, these are not forced marriages. The two young people are usually given a chance to meet and may or may not agree to the match. Because the marriage forms a link between two family groups, the pressure against divorce and separation is great.

## CHINESE

The Chinese are also loyal to the family unit. It is the duty of younger generations to look after elders. The Chinese turn to relations and close friends for help when it is needed. There is great reluctance to go to outsiders or the State. This is partly because of the importance of "saving face" in Chinese culture. Receiving help from outsiders can mean "losing face".

## WEST INDIANS

West Indian families can be like Asian families in providing support for members. But there is not the strong obligation within West Indian culture. Help given often depends more on personal feelings than on a sense of duty.

The background of people in Britain from the Caribbean varies. Most are descended from Africans brought to the Caribbean as slaves. The African family system was quickly broken down by the practice of slavery. Husbands and wives, even parents and children were separated and sold to different plantations. Slave-owners discouraged family units and family life. Slaves were not allowed to marry, and slave fathers were allowed no rights or

The Simms family. Mr and Mrs Simms came to Britain in the early 1950s from Jamaica. Their children were born in the UK. Mrs Simms: "My children bluntly told me they do not feel British. They said to me 'Although we were born here, we don't feel British because we are treated so differently.'" Mrs Simms was the first woman to drive a school bus for the Inner London Education Authority.

duties towards children they produced.

Caribbean family life today still reflects some of the disruption imposed by slavery. Many West Indians live in the conventional nuclear family (father, mother and children), but it is still common for unmarried women to bear children. Women are often the heads and supporters of families. In Britain the proportion of single parents among West Indians (13%) is higher than among the general population (9%). Most single parents in all groups are women (90%).

For Asians, the proportion of single parents is only 1%. It is quite rare for an unmarried Asian girl to become pregnant. This is considered quite shameful in the Asian community. West Indians accept it more readily, because of the historical disruption to families during slavery.

## CONFLICT BETWEEN GENERATIONS

Young people of all nationalities rebel against their parents. For most people this is part of growing-up. The children of ethnic minorities often have extra difficulties. Besides the usual age gap, they may be facing also a clash of cultures.

Most Asian teenagers come from a home where the group and group wishes are more important than the individual. Meanwhile, at school, these young people are being encouraged to think and act for themselves. Many Asian girls are not allowed the freedoms which other girls may have. Asian girls may see girls in Britain going out with boyfriends and eventually choosing a husband. For some Asian girls, the idea of an arranged marriage is upsetting and a source of conflict with their parents.

One 16-year-old daughter of an English mother and Pakistani father begged a court in 1983 to put her in care to avoid an arranged marriage. "My father wants to send me to Pakistan to be married. I want to lead a Western lifestyle and study at a sixth-form college." A High Court granted her appeal.

Young people of ethnic minority background born in the UK have grown up with Western ideas and the values of British culture. These are sometimes in sharp contrast with ideas held by their parents born in more traditional societies.

Young Asians and young West Indians are often not willing to put up with the discrimination which many of their parents felt they simply had to accept. Some young blacks are rebelling against their own ethnic leadership for, as they see it, not standing up enough for minority rights.

## CHILDREN INTO CARE

Ethnic minority families generally make fewer demands on the Social Services than the general population. But an area of concern *is* the disproportionate number of black and mixed-race children coming into the care of the local authorities since the early 1970s.

There are no exact figures available, because records of ethnic origin are either not kept or not released. Some figures were obtained, however, by Soul Kids Campaign. This London-based group wants to find more Caribbean homes for Caribbean-origin children in care. In Wandsworth, in the mid-1970s, nearly half of the children in care were of Caribbean origin. In Wolverhampton nearly a third of children in care were black. (These were mainly of Caribbean origin, but the proportion of Asians has been rising.)

A study of Bradford showed that one child in every fifteen born of mixed parentage was in the care of a local authority. This compared to one in sixty-six for the general population.

Children can come into the care of Social Services Departments for a number of reasons. They may be admitted voluntarily because of unsatisfactory home conditions or if a single parent is unable to cope. Children may be committed into care by the courts because of a history of offences or because they are beyond the control of parents, or because of neglect or ill-treatment by parents.

Many West Indians and Asians think social

David and Jenny Mulchreest are one of many happy mixed marriages in Britain. Jenny's father was born in Bangladesh. Jenny remembers a hurtful experience when taking baby Leo out: "We stopped to look in some shops. An ordinary middle-aged white couple were looking in the same window. As I walked past the man said in a loud voice, 'There are enough of them here already without them breeding'." Jenny expects more painful moments: "I dread the first child making a remark to Leo about his black mother."

◀ Eric Bledman (left) came to Britain from St Lucia in the West Indies at the age of sixteen. He had a strict, disciplined upbringing. "I don't think it did me any harm at all. But it's hard for kids born here to West Indian parents to understand why they don't have all the freedom their white friends have. When I have a kid he's having a West Indian upbringing. If I tell my kid to do something, he's going to do it." Eric has helped out at a youth club giving teenagers who have been in trouble "something to do and somewhere to go". Eric: "A really high proportion of crime is caused by bored kids."

workers take ethnic minority children into care more readily because they have less understanding of and less regard for black families. Another possible factor may be that black families and mixed-race families are under more economic and social stress and this can result in extra problems among some.

Yet another contributing factor may be the fact that so many ethnic minority women work, out of economic necessity. In some areas over 80% of West Indian mothers of pre-school children work, and 50% is quite common. (In the general population only about 20% of mothers with pre-school children work.) The shortage of adequate day-care facilities is an extra strain on these families. (A large proportion of Asian mothers also work: nearly 50% of non-Muslims and 20% of Muslims.)

One reason why ethnic minority families generally make fewer demands on the Social Services is that they are, overall, younger than the whole population. Only about 4% of the ethnic minorities are age 60 or over – compared to 20% of the total UK population. But the numbers of older people are increasing amongst all groups. The black elderly have some special needs and problems beyond the general problems facing the old.

Many of the elderly in ethnic minorities were born in another country (in Africa, the West Indies, the Indian subcontinent, Hong Kong . . . ). In these places, especially in villages and less modern areas, the elderly are held in higher regard than they are in Britain. Older people receive more respect and have more influence in families. Life expectancies are somewhat lower in these areas so there are, in fact, fewer (proportionately) old people. The black elderly in Britain are having to adjust to the much less revered role of older people in the UK.

Ethnic minority workers pay National Insurance Contributions like everyone else and so are entitled to retirement pensions based on those contributions. A problem for some older immigrants is that they have not worked in the UK long enough to qualify for a full pension. They can, in some cases, claim a supplementary pension, but this does restrict their chances for earnings from part-time work. Many older immigrants are on low pensions (about half the standard rate) and yet resist claiming any supplementary pension. They feel a stigma attached to the need to claim. Many elderly blacks are amongst the poorest of elderly people in Britain.

Many black elderly hesitate to attend clubs for the British elderly. Experiences of hostility have left many older immigrants feeling unwelcome. This can mean many older blacks feeling even more isolated than the general retired population.

One old woman described waiting for the lift to her flat: "I was just called by a white man 'Black Bastard'. . . . I wanted the lift to go up and he was there holding it back." Experiences like this make many black elderly wary of mixing with whites, for fear of rejection.

Traditionally, ethnic minorities prefer to look after the elderly in their own homes. Most minority groups share the feeling that it is a disgrace to put elderly people in residential care. It is "like sending them to the moon", according to one Chinese community worker. This is especially true for the Chinese, among whom respect for the elderly is a very strong tradition.

Nevertheless, an increasing number of some ethnic minority old people are being cared for in old people's homes. The few black elderly in a mostly white home often feel quite isolated. In some cases, provision has been made for Afro-Caribbean or Asian food as an alternative menu, but this is not always available. Lambeth Council in London is one that has been making special provisions for the black elderly. These include special ethnic meals available on "meals on wheels". In 1978 Lambeth Council adopted an Equal Opportunities Policy. They set up a unit to carry out positive action to redress any disadvantage to minorities which had evolved in the council's activities.

Types of housing in Britain make it difficult for Asians and other ethnic minorities to care for the old in the traditional way. The Asian Community Action Group in Wandsworth, London has been working on a sheltered housing scheme to try to solve this problem. In some cases, the elderly are feeling the stress. As one Asian elder said: "They are thinking that they are unwanted, undesirable and a burden to the family and society as well."

Among Cypriot families it is also traditional for the elderly to be cared for by their children. An early 1980s survey in Haringey, London showed that many houses belonging to Cypriots were simply not large enough to accommodate elderly relatives adequately. Most older Cypriots do still live with their families, but an increasing number are living on their own.

Language and illiteracy are other problems

Elderly West Indians play dominoes at the Calabash Club in South London. The Club was set up by the Lewisham Community Relations Council.

for many black elderly. A 1981 survey in Birmingham showed that 88% of elderly Asians could not speak English. A more general UK survey in 1975 found that 55% of Asian men and 82% of Asian women over the age of 45 spoke little or no English.

Many black elderly do not even know their rights and entitlements. The 1981 Birmingham survey showed that 64% of elderly Asians had no knowledge of the benefits they could be claiming as pensioners and the services available to them. There is also a great reluctance among many, especially Asians and most particularly the Chinese, to accept help from the State. It is a matter of tradition and pride to stay within the family for support.

All ethnic groups have expressed the need for more day centres for the elderly. Some areas do have these, and some are run on a self-help basis. An example is the Brixton Senior Citizens' Luncheon Club, where West Indian food is served. The club was started in 1973 by West Indians for their own elderly. By 1982 there were 400 members. The club runs activities, outings and crafts. Children from local schools come to entertain. The older people at the club are mainly immigrants who came to Britain in the late 1940s.

# Food

Many high streets in Britain reflect the variety of ethnic groups living here. There are speciality shops selling the vegetables, spices and other foods which minorities use in their cooking. These foods are often bought by the general population as well. There are also many restaurants serving Indian, Greek and other national dishes (over 6,500 Chinese restaurants and take-away shops alone!)

The availability of ethnic food in Britain has widened food horizons. Many people enjoy the adventure of trying new types of dishes. The Jamaican chef at a smart West Indian restaurant in Brixton says that "whites are quite adventurous about Caribbean food if they're eating out in a group." The restaurant speciality of the house is curried goat.

There are courses for people who want to learn to cook ethnic minority dishes themselves. In 1982 the BBC ran a television series on *Indian Cooking*. The Adult Education Institute in Haringey, North London runs courses by a Guyanese woman teaching West Indian, African and Black American cooking. This includes such dishes as ground-nut stew, tuna fish with seaweed, Creole cod, and banana bake. In Southwest London there is a "Memories of China" cooking school.

The diets that ethnic minorities eat are sometimes closely linked to their religious beliefs. This is especially true of people from the Indian subcontinent (an area as large as Europe). Most of the groups in Britain have come from the northern part of the subcontinent, so there are some similarities in what they all eat.

In contrast to "British" diets, Asian diets are high in cereals, roughage and vegetables and low in animal fat and sugar. Nutritionally, this is quite good. Asians believe in the need for a balance of foods, which are described as being either "cold" or "hot". This description has nothing to do with the actual temperature of the food. Foods regarded as "hot" are those high in animal protein or salt. It is believed that these excite the emotions. Sweet, bitter or sour foods are usually considered "cold". These are thought to calm the emotions. The belief is that too much of either hot or cold food unbalances the body and can be a source of illness.

People from the subcontinent in Britain generally eat much less meat than the British. Most Hindus are vegetarian and do not eat meat or fish. Some Sikhs are also strictly vegetarian. Even those Hindus and Sikhs who are not vegetarians will usually not eat pork or beef. Muslims will not eat pork or pork products. They do eat other meats if the animals are killed according to Islamic law. (This "halal" meat has had Allah pronounced over the animal and the animal's throat has been cut quickly so that it bleeds to death). Muslims will eat fish that have fins and scales.

A couple of Jamaican origin shopping in Lewisham, South London. The foods shown – yams (in foreground), breadfruit (round, close to the woman), sweet potatoes and green bananas – are West Indian staples.

A Gujarati woman in Glasgow making chapattis
(wheat pancakes).

Sima Patel puts dinner on the table. The Patel family is originally Gujarati, but has come from Kenya. Indian dishes shown are as follows:
1. Dhokhra, made of yoghurt, chick pea flour and spices.
2. Mixed salad, containing onions, tomatoes, lettuce, carrots and cucumbers.
3. Shak, cooked spiced vegetables.
4. Dahl, lentil soup.
5. Fruit salad with mangoes and oranges.
6. Rice.
7. Dry chicken with curry spices.
8. Chapattis, wheat pancakes.
9. Battered chillis.
10. Dhai Wada, bhaja in yoghurt.

Very strict Hindus and Sikhs do not eat eggs, but other Hindus and Sikhs may. Muslims do not eat eggs. Most adult Asians not raised in Britain dislike the flavour of Western cheeses. Milk and yoghurt are permitted for all Hindus, Sikhs and Muslims. The devout in all three religions do not touch alcohol, but some Westernized Hindus and Sikhs do drink.

Pulses such as chickpeas and lentils are a major source of protein for Asian vegetarian diets. In Britain about ten different types of pulses are used. Vegetables such as carrots, cauliflowers, potatoes, cucumbers and onions are used in the northern Indian subcontinent and so are widely used by Asians here. There are some other vegetables such as sweet

Young Cypriot waiters outside a Greek restaurant in London. There are thousands of ethnic restaurants in Britain, offering Britons the chance to eat an interesting variety of foods. Such Greek specialities as moussaka and kebabs have become familiar favourites.

potatoes and gourds which Indian grocers in Britain supply. Salads may be sprinkled with fresh lemon juice instead of dressing.

Spices are an important part of Asian cooking. Those most widely used are cardamom, cinnamon, cumin, coriander, ginger, turmeric and chilli powder. Children are usually given the same food, but with less spice.

Northern India and Pakistan are mainly wheat growing and eating areas. Bangladesh is mainly rice eating. The main staple food for Sikhs and Hindus from the Indian Punjab and Muslims from Pakistan is chapattis – a type of wheat pancake. Hindus or Muslims from Gujarat may eat either chapattis or rice. Muslims from Bangladesh eat rice as their staple.

Asians in Britain from the Indian Punjab use ghee (a clarified butter) as their main fat. Those from Gujarat use groundnut or mustard oil and some ghee. Pakistanis use ghee or groundnut oil. Bangladeshis use groundnut or mustard oil and a little ghee.

Breakfast for Asians in Britain may be quite Western, with packaged cereals and toast. But evening meals are often still traditional. Chapattis or rice may supply about half of the bulk of the meal. Dishes of vegetable or meat curry may have yoghurt and pickles on the side. Fresh fruit and tea may be served after. The tradition is to put all dishes in the centre of the table and for people to help themselves through the meal.

Hindus, Sikhs and Muslims may all fast at some times. Hindus and Sikhs decide personally to fast, sometimes on major religious festivals. Muslims are required to fast from dawn to sunset during the month of Ramadan.

# Health

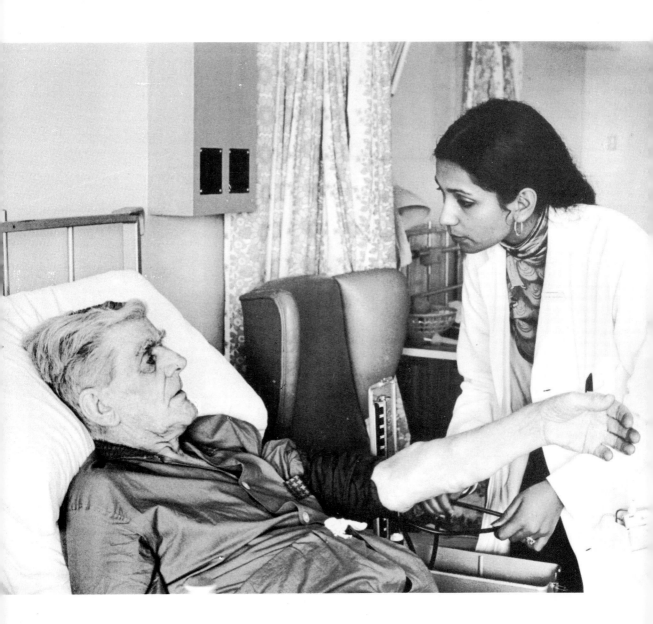

Ethnic minorities in Britain face much the same health hazards and problems as everyone else. There are, however, some health issues which affect them especially.

## SICKLE-CELL ANAEMIA

Sickle-cell anaemia is identified with black people who live in the Caribbean, Britain and the USA. It is an inherited and as yet incurable blood disease affecting about one in every three hundred black people. It is *not* an infectious disease. It is *not* something you can "catch". It is passed from one generation to the next along with other physical traits.

The disease affects red blood cells. Pain may be slight or entry to hospital may be necessary. The Sickle-Cell Centre at Willesden General Hospital in London gives help for those affected.

## RICKETS AND OSTEOMALACIA

A health problem particularly affecting Asian communities is Vitamin D deficiency. In extreme cases, this leads to rickets (deformed bones) in children and osteomalacia (softening of bones) in adults. Vitamin D is essential for bones to grow properly and strong. The vitamin is taken in by the body from sunlight on the skin and from some foods.

Those living in Britain on traditional diets may not be getting enough of the vitamin either from the sun or from food. Natural food sources of vitamin D (liver, eggs and oily fish) are not eaten by vegetarian Hindus and Sikhs. Some processed foods (eg margarine) are fortified with vitamin D – but these are not part of most British Asian diets either.

A survey published in 1982 showed that rickets and osteomalacia are a much bigger health problem than expected amongst poorer Asian families in a number of cities. The Department of Health then launched a national campaign. 5-10% of Asian children in Britain now suffer from rickets – mainly in northern cities. (Rickets was a problem among poor white communities up until the 1940s.)

◀ Dr Bhupinder Kaur Sandhu came to Britain from India at the age of eleven. Over a third of all the hospital doctors in the UK were born overseas (mostly in the Indian subcontinent). Ethnic minority doctors, nurses, and other staff play a vital part in keeping Britain's National Health Service running. But immigrant doctors do face discrimination. They tend to be given posts in the least well-equipped hospitals and departments (such as geriatrics – treating the very old) that are not popular with English doctors. Bhupinder: "I think the initial reaction of some patients is 'perhaps he or she isn't as good as a white doctor'... one hopes to make them realize that you are concerned about their health and they are a person to you, regardless of the colour difference between you."

# Housing

Britain's ethnic minorities show a somewhat different pattern of housing from the population as a whole. In 1980 about 54% of households in the UK overall were owner-occupiers. The figure was 70% for Asians and 36% for West Indians. Only 15% of UK households were renting from private landlords – compared to 20% of Asian households and 14% of West Indian households. In recent years there has been a shift of West Indian households into public housing, but the Asians have not followed this. While 31% of UK households rented from a local authority or housing association, only 10% of Asian households did so. This compared to 50% of West Indians.

The quality of the housing which ethnic minorities have been able to buy tends to be amongst the nation's poorest. Minorities are much more likely to be in overcrowded housing and sharing some basic amenities. Older, run-down inner city housing was bought, because this was all that many could afford. When immigrants arrived from Asia, Africa and the West Indies they could not fulfil the residence qualifications of most local authorities for council housing. Their choice was either to buy old inner city houses or to rent privately.

It was, in fact, Asian *manual* workers who were (at the time of late 1970s surveys) more likely to be owner-occupiers than Asian professionals. This is the reverse of the general picture for the British population.

A Political and Economic Planning (PEP) study published in 1975 said that Asian and West Indian households were disadvantaged in their access to public housing. The report found that Asians and West Indians had to wait longer before being rehoused and were given lower-quality accommodation. While local authorities were not consciously discriminating as a matter of policy, practices worked to the disadvantage of minority groups. There were, for example, too few four- and five-bedroom properties. Therefore, minority applicants, tending to have larger than average households, needed to wait longer. The report concluded that council housing policies have increased the concentration of ethnic minorities in inner city areas. These are the areas of poorest housing.

Bengali children in London's East End. Many ethnic
minority families are concentrated in older, inner-city
housing. Poor housing and overcrowding are
contributors to such "diseases of poverty" as
tuberculosis. The rate of TB in the East London
borough of Tower Hamlets is six times the national
average and causing much concern. Asians are only
20% of the Tower Hamlets population – but were
nearly 40% of notified TB cases in the borough in the
early 1980s.

# Languages

The great mix of immigrants to Britain has brought a variety of languages. In 1978 the Inner London Education Authority discovered 131 (!) different languages spoken by pupils. Over 80% of children with a language other than English as their mother tongue spoke one of the following twelve: Bengali, Turkish, Greek, Spanish, Gujarati, Punjabi, Italian, Urdu, Chinese, French, Arabic or Portuguese.

There are other cities besides London with a large number of languages spoken. In Leicester these languages include Latvian, Ukrainian, Polish, Chinese, Punjabi, Gujarati, Bengali and Italian. Even in smaller areas there is often a surprising range. In Bexley, Kent, there are no fewer than seventeen languages and dialects spoken as a mother tongue.

## VOLUNTARY LANGUAGE CLASSES

Ethnic groups want to keep their languages in use by the next generation. Children (especially those born in Britain) sometimes resist learning the mother tongue of the parents.

Most teaching of mother tongues takes place in voluntary part-time classes. Many of these classes face problems of overcrowded premises, shortages of materials, and difficulties of transport. Some classes are held in schools after school hours. Others use temples, mosques, churches and community centres.

Italian and Spanish classes are mostly paid for by those governments. Nearly three-

---

### Indian, Pakistani and Bangladeshi Languages in Britain

There are *hundreds* of different languages on the Indian subcontinent (and *hundreds* more dialects). Most Asians in Britain from the subcontinent speak one or more of these six languages:

*Punjabi:* spoken by Indians and Pakistanis from the Punjab. *Mirpuri* is a dialect of Punjabi spoken by those from Mirpur.

*Gujarati:* spoken by Indians from Gujarat. *Kutchi* is a dialect of Gujarati spoken by those from Northern Gujarat.

*Pashto:* spoken by Pakistanis from the N.W. Frontier Province.

*Bengali:* spoken by those from Bangladesh. *Sylheti* is a dialect of Bengali spoken by most Bangladeshis in Britain.

*Hindi:* the formal, educated language of northern India.

*Urdu:* the formal, educated language of Pakistan.

---

### Chinese Languages in Britain

About 70% of the Chinese in the UK speak *Cantonese*, while 25% speak *Hakka*. (Both groups are mainly from Hong Kong.) The rest are northerners from Taiwan and mainland China, and migrants from S.E. Asia whose native dialects are *Fujianese* and *Chao Chou*.

---

Pamela Gupta (right) and friend outside their primary  school. Pamela was born in Derby and has lived there all of her eight years. She speaks English at school, but Hindi at home. Her parents own a shop. She has a sister, Suman, and two brothers, Sudheer and Sanjay. On Sundays Pamela goes to a temple school to learn to write Hindi. She wrote this as an example:

हाथ साफ कर

"Wash Your hands"

quarters of Chinese language classes are provided with books from the Hong Kong government office in the UK. The Chinese have about fifty language classes across the UK. Most teachers for all of these classes are volunteers. Fees, if charged at all, are very low. The Cheung's Clansmen Charity Association (for those Chinese with the surname Cheung) runs Chinese language classes in Soho for caterers' children.

Shortage of teachers for voluntary classes has been a problem in some areas. As of 1982, there were no facilities for young people from ethnic minorities to specially train to teach minority languages. The Commission for Racial Equality has been working towards setting up such training at eight teacher training institutions.

One reason for teaching mother tongues is to encourage a pride in ethnic cultural heritage. Sometimes language teaching is related to religious studies. Since 1966, two mosques in Preston, Lancashire have held religious classes in both Urdu and Arabic. There are now nearly one thousand students.

Families without access to classes often encourage children to speak their mother tongue at home. But this does not keep alive the tradition of reading and writing. A 1981 Leicester Council for Community Relations report showed that although most Asian children could *speak* their mother tongue, less than a fifth could read and write it. 95% of the Asian parents who were asked thought it was important for their children to know an Asian language.

## MOTHER TONGUES IN REGULAR SCHOOLS

The Commission for Racial Equality is urging that more of the languages spoken at home by ethnic minorities should be taught in modern language departments at state schools. This would raise the status of these languages in the eyes of both ethnic and native UK pupils – and provide a link between home and school. The CRE points out that these languages should be regarded not as "foreign" but as *community* languages of the UK.

A National Union of Teachers policy statement in 1981 also asked schools to give higher status to ethnic minority languages. The NUT says that mother tongue teaching should be available for all primary pupils.

Research shows that children taught basic skills in their mother tongue make greater progress than children taught only in English. As the NUT says, "Pupils are slower to progress with school work if their use of their mother tongue is not accepted and catered for." There is a growing recognition that these languages are a valuable resource which children bring into schools. In 1982 the BBC began broadcasting a schools programme called *Mother Tongue Story*. A simple folktale was told first in English – and then in Punjabi, Urdu, Hindi, Gujarati, Sylhetic, standard Bengali and Cantonese.

The NUT also says that all secondary students should be able to study minority languages like Urdu and Gujarati to examination level. The Schools Council has been looking at possible exams in Hindi, Urdu and Modern Greek as an encouragement to mother tongue teaching.

In 1983, for the first time, ILEA appointed 14 teachers to teach the main immigrant languages (including Gujarati, Urdu, Greek and Bengali). ILEA also recruited an inspector of the teaching of mother tongue languages.

The secretary of the National Association for Multicultural Education (NAME) has said: "Apart from the help it gives to children who find it easier to learn their mother tongue language and English at the same time when they are young, it makes an enormous contribution to race relations."

## WEST INDIAN CREOLE

Many West Indian children speak an English-based Creole as a home language. This is regarded by some people as just a dialect of English. Others regard Creole languages as quite separate. One main difference is that Jamaican Creole does not regularly indicate past tenses of verbs in the way that standard

The "Bilingual Under Fives" project was set up in 1978 by the Inner London Education Authority to help young bilingual children learn to use English as their second language. Materials include stories and recipes from a variety of cultures. Face puzzles, showing different ethnic groups, are popular starters for discussion.

"Nou, Breda pik up iz myuuzik man an wen ing riich about a aaf mailz tu di King giet . . ."
"Now Brother picked up his music men and when he reached about a half a mile from the King's gate . . ."

English does. Many West Indian children have problems in UK schools in understanding standard English and in being understood. Here is a sentence in Jamaican Creole, and its translation into standard English:

TEACHING ENGLISH

While encouraging mother tongues, it is also important for ethnic minorities to know the host country language of English. Poor skills in English are a serious disadvantage, especially

39

when looking for jobs. The PEP report of 1976 found that about 40% of Asian men and 60% of Asian women spoke English only slightly or not at all. The figure was highest for Pakistani women – 77%.

The Commission for Racial Equality estimated in the late 1970s that there were over 200,000 adults in Britain speaking English slightly or not at all. Most were from Asia, but some were from Southern Europe as well. A 1981 report by the National Association for Teaching English as a Second Language said that nearly half a million adults from ethnic minority communities in Britain needed more help with learning to speak, read and write English.

There are some industrial language training courses which teach English to workers at the workplace. These classes take place on site, mainly in work time. The National Centre for Industrial Language Training (NCILT) was set up in 1974. Projects were being run in over 200 companies by the late 1970s.

_____ ETHNIC PRESS _____

There is a sizeable press published in Britain for and by ethnic minorities. The number of Asian language newspapers is, in fact, increasing – although the number of readers is shrinking (as younger Asians grow up reading English).

*Daily Jang* has been printed in London since 1971 for the approximately 300,000 Urdu-speaking Pakistanis in the UK. Kazi Ashraf of *Daily Jang* has said: "The younger generation cannot read or write Urdu. In time our readership could die out and we may be – perish the thought – publishing entirely in English."

There are about 35 Asian language periodicals in the UK for the two million people of Asian origin living here. This includes nine Urdu papers, eight Bengali, six Punjabi, four Gujarati, three Hindi, two Chinese, two Tamil and one Telegu (a south Indian language). (There are about twenty more fringe political papers in Asian languages in Britain as well.)

Britain's only Chinese language daily newspaper printed in the UK is called *Sing Tao*. A satellite transmits information from Hong Kong to an ultra-modern printing plant just outside London. Daily circulation is over 10,000.

There are three weekly newspapers, two monthly magazines and a yearbook specifically for the West Indian community. *Bogle L'Ouverture* began as a black publishing company and black bookshop. There is even a company called Ebony Greeting Cards formed by West Indians to produce "ethnically relevant" greeting cards for the black population.

Bradford. A voluntary language class learning ▶ Punjabi on a Sunday.

# Education

Emmanuel Josiah, a Nigerian, is Director of the African Arts in Education project. He visits UK schools with a range of West African instruments, costumes and other artefacts. People in Britain can learn much about other countries and cultures from the ethnic minority people who are here.

A 1974 National Child Development Study of 16-year-olds found that first generation immigrant young people from *all* areas (including Ireland and Europe) tend to do worse at school than children born in Britain. This is accounted for by problems with language and adjusting to a new country and culture. But many young black people *born in Britain* seem to be facing extra problems as well.

The Department of Education and Science set up a commission of inquiry in the late 1970s on how ethnic minorities were faring in the UK educational system. A survey of school leavers in six authorities found that only 9% of West Indians achieved an O level or its CSE equivalent in English, compared with 21% of Asians and 29% of other leavers. In Mathematics, only 5% of West Indians achieved O level or its equivalent – compared with 20% of Asians and 19% of other leavers. Only 1% of West Indians went on to full-time degree courses, compared with 5% of Asians and 4% of other leavers.

The report suggested no single cause for why West Indians especially have been having difficulties. It did suggest that inappropriate teaching and curriculum were factors, as were negative teacher attitudes. Many teachers had low academic expectations of West Indian pupils – and this seemed a discouragement. The commission called for more black teachers and multi-cultural curricula to encourage all children from all backgrounds.

Some black university students gave evidence to the commission. They said that West Indians have to play down their colour and cultural background in order to succeed in British schools. Black students also said there was a tendency for West Indians to be put at the "bottom" automatically – whatever their real potential.

West Indian parents have complained that too many of their children are being sent to schools for the educationally subnormal. The commission was unable to confirm or deny this claim. It did suggest that some under-achievement by West Indians seemed rooted in the pre-school years. Day-care provision for the under-fives was inadequate and inappropriate for the needs of West Indian families.

A disproportionate number of West Indian women have to work because of economic circumstances. Nearly twice as many West Indian as white men work night shifts. The West Indian community also has proportionately more one-parent families. The commission's suggestion was that some West Indian parents have less time to spend with their children, and this puts those children at a disadvantage in learning at school.

An early 1980s survey of over 1000 children in a Midlands town showed that at the age of five, West Indian children do just as well in tests as other racial groups. But from the age of seven, white children start to pull ahead. The reasons why older West Indian children as a group do not do as well in school may be partly rooted in a less settled family life. In the survey's pre-school sample, only 59% of the West Indian children lived in households where the father was present and only 37% where the parents were married.

"Supplementary" or Saturday schools have sprung up in many inner cities since the late 1970s. These are to meet the religious, social or educational needs of ethnic minority groups that are not always being met in regular schools. One supplementary school for young West Indians in south London was set up by a parents' association. The association also runs a youth club and a mother and toddlers group, helps teenagers looking for jobs, and takes a yearly group holiday to the West Indies. The Saturday school has about 100 children aged 2-18, with eight members of staff – mostly unpaid. Three subjects are taught: English, maths and drawing or artwork. Children have much individual help and attention. Parents pay a small monthly fee. The school is to give the children extra help in basic skills.

Ethnic minorities have come into conflict with British schools over the way pupils dress, what pupils eat and other traditions. Usually, UK schools have insisted on minorities

In late 1982 thousands of Sikhs rallied for the right to wear turbans in all British schools, institutions and places of work. A Birmingham headmaster had refused to admit a Sikh pupil with a turban. The Federation of Sikh Organizations has been lobbying the Home Office and MPs. There have been conflicts as well over Sikhs on motorbikes refusing to take off their turbans to wear crash helmets. Turbans are of special importance to the Sikhs, but the majority community has not always understood this.

adapting to British ways and customs. But some authorities have tried to provide for the right of minorities to be "different". An example is Bradford. A new policy began in late 1982 making special provision for the city's 12,000 Asian pupils. "Halal" meat is now available for school meals. Sikh religious bracelets are now allowed. Girls have separate physical education. *Imams* (priests) can come into

schools to conduct Friday Muslim prayers. Minority parents are being told of their rights to withdraw children from school for religious festivals, if wanted. The British chairman of the educational services committee said: "For the past 20 years we have been sitting in City Hall identifying the views of the Asian community. In the last two years we've gone out to talk to them – and found they had completely different views from those we perceived."

Despite these changes, in 1983 Muslims in Bradford wanted to take over five schools in the city in which their children were the vast majority. Muslim parents wanted to add Islamic religious education as well as the Arabic language to the timetable. According to the 1944 Education Act, religious minorities have a right to run their own schools. Bradford's council has been against such segregation. They favour state schools making greater progress to meet the needs of Muslim and other minority pupils.

Berkshire was another education authority to plan reforms in 1982. The plan called for the training of all staff about ways to fight racism; for action to appoint more black teachers, governors and officers; education for all pupils giving a black and Third World perspective as well as a "British" one; and reform of the school system which unconsciously discriminates against black children. Policy statements or discussion papers on multi-cultural education have been published also by other authorities, such as ILEA, Derbyshire, Avon, Leeds, Bedfordshire, Croydon and Manchester.

In 1982 the Inner London Education Authority voted to go ahead with stronger policies on multi-ethnic education. A special Equal Opportunities Unit was created to encourage more ethnic minority staff. Schools are being asked to develop policies to deal with racism. Staff are being given advice on dealing with racial incidents. ILEA is also asking exam boards to end discrimination against or disadvantage for pupils from ethnic minority groups.

Many schools have been trying to achieve a

Bradford. The few Muslim boys in one school have a separate session with the Head while Christian R.I. is taught. The 42,000 Muslim community in Bradford has been very divided about the proposal of the Muslim Parents' Association to buy five city schools and make these Islamic. The Association wants children of Pakistani and Bangladeshi origin to keep their "identity". The local Asian Youth Movement opposes the idea of separate schools, saying that they would become targets for racists. Young Asians also argue that employers would be likely to discriminate against former pupils of Islamic schools.

more multi-cultural curriculum. At Tulse Hill comprehensive school near Brixton in south London about half of the boys are black (ranging from West Indian to Asian to Turkish to Chilean). That variety is reflected in what is taught. The school's curriculum has become much more multi-ethnic since the early 1970s. The head of religious studies (himself black) includes Hinduism, Islam and other religions besides Christianity. Heroes studied include black leaders such as Gandhi and Martin Luther King.

Oldknow School, Birmingham, held a "Festival of Cultures" in 1982. For three weeks there were in-school workshops on Indian, African and Caribbean arts and crafts. Local ethnic minority people helped to teach pupils about mirrorwork in Rajasthan, Amahric (Ethiopian script), chain stitch embroidery, engraving, batik – as well as Afro-Caribbean food and dancing, and the Indian musical instrument, the sitar.

# Employment

Ethnic minorities complain that they are the last to be hired for good jobs and the first to be fired in hard times. The facts suggest that there is some reason for concern.

A national survey in 1977 found that 41% of

Mohammed Ibrahim runs a small corner store in Bradford. He works a hard 84-hour week, for a very modest living. "It's all right," he says. "It's a respectable job and independent." Ibrahim is a university graduate in economics and history. He is one of many ethnic minority people working at a level less skilled than their qualifications. A survey of over 500 retail and service businesses in Bradford, Leicester and Southall found that 60% of the Asian traders were graduates, compared to only 9% of whites.

white working men were in professional, managerial and other non-manual work. This compared to just 11% of West Indian working men, and 26% of Asians. Job levels were lower too amongst women. A third of white working women were in unskilled and semi-skilled manual work, compared with half of West Indian working women and nearly half of Asian working women.

Overall, ethnic minorities do tend to have poorer jobs and earn less than the white working population. This is not explained by "blacks having poorer qualifications". The 1976 PEP report *Facts of Racial Disadvantage* noted

that 79% of white men with degrees were in professional/managerial jobs, compared with 31% of Asian/Afro-Caribbean men with those qualifications.

A Nottingham study in the years 1977-79 tested over one hundred firms. Nearly half rejected written applications for white-collar jobs from Asian and Afro-Caribbean origin candidates, in preference for white applicants. (All applicants had directly comparable qualifications and experience.)

1981 reports suggested that ethnic minorities are more likely than whites to be working in manufacturing industries in which jobs are declining. Asian workers especially are in declining sectors such as clothing, textiles, metalwork and foundries. Ethnic minorities are also more likely than whites to be on shift work.

Ethnic minorities are disproportionately represented in poorer jobs – and also amongst the unemployed. As general unemployment rises, ethnic minority unemployment rises even faster. From early 1979 to early 1980 ethnic minority unemployment rose *four times* as fast as overall unemployment. From early 1980 to early 1981 ethnic minority unemployment rose by 83% – compared to 66% for unemployment overall. The rate for young blacks born in Britain increased by much more – 112%.

Surveys suggest that it may be two or three times harder for young blacks to find jobs than it is for their white peers. A late 1982 report showed that 60% of young Afro-Caribbean people available for work in the 16-20 age range were without jobs. This compared to 40% for whites and Asians. The Opinion Research Centre survey also showed that 25% of blacks and 19% of Asians thought that their colour made it harder to get work. Half the whites thought that some employers were racially prejudiced. The Chairman of the Commission for Racial Equality said that: "The time has come for all employers to face the fact of discrimination and take effective action to end it."

A 1982 CRE survey found nearly 60% of employers discriminating against young black people applying for jobs. Black and white people (of the same age and qualifications) applied by telephone for jobs advertised in South London local papers. In 26% of cases the white was offered an interview while the black applicant was rejected. In a further 32% of cases the black applicant was told that the vacancy was filled or that he or she was unsuitable. Meanwhile, white testers were being sent application forms or otherwise given more favourable treatment.

A Fabian Society pamphlet in 1980 urged Britain to adopt some of the affirmative action or "positive discrimination" used in the USA to help ethnic minorities. In 1981 the Confederation of Indian Organizations also called for more positive discrimination and training schemes for young unemployed blacks. "Positive discrimination" in favour of minorities is regarded by some as unfair.

Another controversial idea is whether or not there should be "monitoring". This means counting the numbers of ethnic minority people within an organization to see if they are fairly represented. Monitoring has been successful in some large firms. The CRE supports this system.

In early 1982 the CRE urged local authorities to take positive action in the employment of and provision of services to ethnic minorities. About twenty local authorities had already taken some form of action ranging from setting up a race relations committee to starting a formal

Joan Arboine is in her early twenties. She came to ▶ Britain from Jamaica at the age of fifteen, to join her parents. She has eight O levels, three CSEs, an ONC in business and management studies and is studying at evening class for A levels in law and government. She has had three jobs since leaving school but is now unemployed. Joan: "Blacks face two sets of problems. It's not just getting the job, but the sticks you get once you're inside. Every job, once I've proved myself, I can't get any further. There is just a brick wall there all the time. There seems to be a limit to how far you're allowed to extend yourself. It's very humiliating after you've done all the work, got extra qualifications and then find that there's nothing at the end of the rainbow . . . . You never know what you're fighting. It's like shadow boxing."

equal opportunities programme. Also in 1982, the government ordered an experimental census within the Civil Service, to see how many people from ethnic minorities work there.

The BBC, in late 1982, was considering monitoring the racial origin of new staff. Governors had dropped the idea of asking existing employees to supply details of origin. It was felt that staff would not be happy about filling in the forms. A BBC spokesman emphasizes: "We are an equal opportunity employer, encouraging people of all groups to apply."

Racial discrimination in employment has been illegal since the 1976 Race Relations Act. The Commission for Racial Equality conducts formal investigations and can take action to enforce the law. For example, in late 1982 a Midlands tractor firm was ordered to stop discriminating against black job seekers. Concern began when it was noted that only about ten of the workforce of seven thousand were Asian or Afro-Caribbean – despite many ethnic minority people in the city.

The CRE also helps individuals to take their cases to Industrial Tribunals. For example, in 1982 a tribunal ruled that a West Indian nurse had not been short-listed for promotion in a private hospital because of her colour.

Ethnic minorities are themselves trying to improve their employment opportunities. The Black Trade Union Solidarity Movement was launched in 1982. This aims to organize black workers and press for more action by unions on minority problems. The co-ordinator has said: "We have realized that things aren't going to change for black people unless they change things for themselves."

# ONE CITY: BEDFORD

About a third of Bedford's population was either born overseas or has parents who were born overseas. One main local employer is a brick company founded in 1936. After the Second World War the local brick industry was short of workers. As in other areas of Britain, people were needed to do work that British people were either not available or unwilling to do. The brick company opened a recruitment office in Naples, Italy in 1951 and a number of Italian workers came. These Italians were not popular with locals in Bedford.

The conditions in which Italian immigrants lived during the 1950s were appalling. Rents were high and there were stories of two workers on different shifts sharing the same bed. There were cases of over forty people sharing one house; each room housed a whole family or four single men.

In 1960 the mayor was quoted as saying of "these voluble and highly excitable" Italian immigrants: " . . . They pack into houses like sardines . . . . In our schools English children are being held back . . . our maternity wards are overflowing with foreign mums . . ." Anti-immigrant remarks (against whites as well as blacks) are not new!

By the early 1960s some immigrants from Pakistan and India had arrived in Bedford. The Ministry of Labour suggested to the brick company that these immigrants might be an alternative labour supply to the Italians. By the end of the 1970s, Asians were a quarter of the workforce on the company's Bedfordshire sites.

Britain's ethnic minority workers are still largely concentrated in the manufacturing industries which first needed them. Many of these workers are still in the essential but most unpleasant and poorly paid jobs which the British did not want to do.

Housing is still a problem for this latest group of immigrants, the Asians. There are still problems of harassment by landlords and overcrowding because of high rents.

Bedford. Asian and Italian employees at a chocolate factory have the chance to learn English. The firm co-operates with the local education authority. Classes are held in the factory for one hour every day, four days a week – half in company time, half in employees' own time.

A Sikh worker at the brick company in Bedford. About three-quarters of all Asians in Bedford are Sikhs from the Indian Punjab.

# Prejudice and Racism

People often have a natural fear of the "unknown". This may include "outsiders" who look somewhat different, dress somewhat differently, eat somewhat different food, speak a different language and/or have a different religion. These "outsiders" may be misunderstood and perhaps disliked just

"4 MILLION MEN, WOMEN AND CHILDREN DIED IN AUSCHWITZ. YOU MIGHT HAVE BEEN ONE." The sign was part of an exhibition brought from the Auschwitz Concentration Camp in Poland. (This camp was one of a number used by the German Nazis to murder Jews and others during the Second World War.) The exhibition was shown in London's East End in 1983. Organizers have been alarmed at growing racism among some young people in Britain. The horrors of the camp show just where racism can lead. In the Depression of the 1930s people blamed the Jews. Their windows were broken, they were assaulted – and finally millions were killed. In Britain in the 1970s and '80s mainly Asians have become victims of racial assaults.

because they are unfamiliar and "different". We support *our* football team, *our* country. Outsiders may be seen as a threat to *us, our* homes and *our* jobs.

When times are hard and jobs are in short supply, there is often a rise in feeling against those easily singled out as "different". People at the bottom of society feel least secure and are most likely to want to "lash out" at "someone".

The word "scapegoat" comes from an old Hebrew ritual. A live goat was taken and all the sins and guilt of the people were put on to it. The goat was then sacrificed. So the phrase "finding a scapegoat" means blaming someone else for our own difficulties and misfortunes. Often the scapegoat chosen by the majority is some ethnic minority. In the Depression of the 1930s it was the Jews who were blamed. In the difficulties of the 1970s and 1980s Asians in Britain have become victims.

The first detailed study of racial violence faced by Bengalis in London's East End was published in 1978. The report noted over one hundred assaults – knifings, muggings, stonings, air-gun attacks . . .

In 1980 Islington Council drew up a list of racial attacks in that area of London. These included assaults with iron bars, a stabbing, harassment of schoolchildren, stone-throwing and other intimidation.

The racism of recent years has not only affected Asians. In 1980 a deputation from the Board of Deputies of British Jews met the Home Secretary. They expressed worry about attacks on Jewish synagogues, schools and businesses.

The Home Office's 1981 report on racial violence urged victims of racialist attacks to report them to the police. Many attacks are unreported, possibly because minorities feel that the police are not concerned.

In early 1982 the Runnymede Trust (a charity promoting education on race relations) called for new measures to combat racial violence. The Home Office admitted that such attacks were common and on the increase. A junior minister said that the government was determined to tackle "this ugly disease". SHELTER, the housing aid charity, also published a report in 1982, saying that not enough was being done.

By the early 1980s a vigilante-style method of dealing with assaults had begun in London. A group called the East London Workers Against Racism (ELWAR) began working in patrols of six to ten people. They visit and assist Asian families who ask for help.

In one of the families helped by ELWAR in 1982, the Bengali father had come to Britain in

A funeral procession in East London for a Pakistani family. Mrs Paveen Khan and her three children, aged eleven, ten and two, died in a fire in their house in 1981. Police know the fire was started deliberately, with petrol. Such racial attacks, against Asians especially, are a worrying trend in some areas.

the early 1960s. In 1979 he had moved with his family into a ground-floor flat in a decaying council block in East London. Attackers had twice tried to set the flat on fire. The front door had been knocked down by a white youth, the windows had been smashed by bricks fifteen times, and the family had all been personally assaulted. ELWAR members began a vigil at the home and went door-to-door to neighbouring flats. One neighbour brought her son, who had admitted breaking windows, to apologise to the Bengali family. The Bengali father said that, with ELWAR members patrolling, "for the first time in two years my family and I feel safe".

Ethnic minority leaders appreciate ELWAR trying to help families, but worry that it is not a real solution to racial attacks. As one leader said: "What happens when they move out?" The police feel that such do-it-yourself policing could provoke more trouble.

In early 1983 councillors in Liverpool voted to evict council house tenants who have been guilty of racial harassment.

Since the late 1960s several organizations against black immigrants have been active in Britain. One organization, the National Front, is a legally constituted political party. They have been putting up candidates for

Linette Simms (left) came from Jamaica in 1953. She shares a joke with her English neighbour. Linette remembers applying for an ambulance driving job in the 1960s. In the interview she was asked what she would do if she called at a home and the patient refused to come with her because of her skin. She said she would never leave a patient because of that. Linette: "I told my children, 'Marry who you like – black, white, pink, green, red, who you like.' Everyone are the same, irrespective to colour. If only people could accept people as they are, it would be a better world . . ."

parliamentary and council elections. Their share of the total national vote was just 3.6% in 1970, down to less than 1.5% in 1979, and much less than 1% in the 1983 General Election.

National Front policies include wanting to deport all coloured immigrants and their descendants to their countries of origin. A survey after the 1979 General Election showed that 88% of all those polled wanted to see the party banned. This included 79% of whites as well as 97% of Afro-Caribbeans and 96% of Asians. In a free, democratic society people should be allowed to express their views. But should a party be allowed which is trying to stir up hatred against minority people? Other organizations with similar views to the Front

include the National Party, the National Democratic Party, the British Movement, and the British National Party.

The conflict between allowing people freedom to express opinions and the need to stop racist activity has been seen in the problem over marches. Racist groups have planned marches and a number of these have been banned. The Public Order Act of 1936 allows for banning a march if it is considered that this would lead to serious public disorder. Such a banning order has to be confirmed by the Home Secretary. In 1980 the Chief Constable of the West Midlands applied for an order to stop an anti-immigrant group marching through an area of Birmingham and West Bromwich heavily populated by blacks. He said: "While we favour freedom of assembly we urge that a march must be banned which is bound to stir up fear and bad feeling." Groups such as the Paddington Campaign Against Racism and the Anti-Nazi League have held counter-demonstrations against marches by anti-immigrant organizations.

"All London Teachers Against Racism and Facism" (ALTARF) was established in 1978. It publishes discussion pamphlets and resources to encourage anti-racist teaching in schools.

# Race Relations Acts

There was much open discrimination against black immigrants in the 1950s and '60s. Notices saying "NO COLOURED" were familiar outside private rented housing and other places.

In 1965 the first Race Relations Act was passed. This made it unlawful to discriminate against people because of their colour, race or national origin in such public places as restaurants, pubs, cinemas, swimming pools and public transport. The Act also said it was an offence to stir up hatred against a minority group. A Race Relations Board was set up to receive complaints from individuals about discrimination. This Board could enquire into cases and try to reach agreement between parties.

Another Act was passed in 1968. This made discrimination illegal also in most cases of housing, employment and advertising. The 1968 Act also set up the Community Relations Commission to work for better racial harmony.

Lily Yau, aged nine, was born in London and has lived in the Chinese area near Piccadilly Circus all her life. Her grandparents' business is importing Chinese video-tapes. Lily speaks Cantonese at home and English with her school friends. Race Relations Acts have encouraged more mixing of different racial groups, and this can help people to understand each other better.

The Commission pressed the government for stronger measures to prevent discrimination and punish those who break the law.

A third Race Relations Act followed in 1976, to make the law against discrimination stronger still. This Act increased the legal protection of minorities in such areas as jobs, housing and education. "Racial discrimination" was widened to include *indirect* discrimination (where conditions or requirements are set which have the effect of keeping out some racial groups without good reason). Another of the changes was to bring clubs into the scope of the law. It became illegal for a club of more than 25 members to refuse membership on the grounds of colour or race.

The new 1976 Act also helped individual complaints. Under the old Act, every complaint went to the Race Relations Board. The 1976 Act gave individuals direct access to the courts. Complaints about jobs go directly to an industrial court called a tribunal. Victims may be awarded financial compensation and given a recommended course of action to put things right. Other complaints (on housing, etc) go to county courts. Damages may be awarded, including awards for injured feelings, and an order against the discrimination.

Another aspect of the 1976 Act is that it allows and encourages local education authorities to take special steps to help minorities.

There are some situations not covered by the 1976 Act. For example, it is *not* against the law to discriminate on racial grounds for employment in a private house. It is also *not* unlawful to discriminate where the characteristics of a particular racial group are a genuine qualification for the job (for example, Chinese waiter wanted for Chinese restaurant). It is also *not* against the law to discriminate on racial grounds in disposing of premises where a landlord or a near relative of the landlord lives on the premises. Discrimination is also allowed on racial grounds for fostering children, or for care of children or others in a private house.

Each of the Race Relations Acts has been a step towards the aim that all people in Britain should have equality of opportunity regardless of the colour of their skin, or where they are from. Of course, laws are made to control what people do, not what people feel or think. However, laws do have an effect on public attitudes. By discouraging racial prejudice in what people *do*, the law is also making *attitudes* of prejudice less acceptable.

# Commission for Racial Equality

A Saturday "career session" organized by the Bradford Community Relations Council. People (especially from ethnic minorities) could meet and talk with employers in a variety of fields. There are about 105 local Community Relations Councils throughout Britain, which run many types of projects – from playgroups to hostels for homeless teenagers. The Councils are involved with housing and employment problems, help with legal advice, and youth work. Support for the Councils comes from such sources as the Commission for Racial Equality, local education authorities, and the Department of Employment.

The 1976 Race Relations Act ended both the Race Relations Board and the Community Relations Commission. These were replaced by a single organization called the Commission for Racial Equality (CRE).

The CRE has been given much stronger powers. The Race Relations Board could only take action on individual complaints, but the CRE can look to see where discrimination exists. Businesses may be required to produce documents and witnesses to help with any investigation. If an enquiry does suggest that an employer (or anyone else) *is* discriminating,

the Commission can serve a non-discrimination notice. The CRE can require proof that changes have been made and that the notice is being followed. While the Commission itself cannot investigate individual complaints, it does help people to prepare and conduct their cases.

The CRE is more than an agency to help enforce the law. It works in other ways to try to promote good race relations. There are booklets and other publications about ethnic minorities. The CRE has links with minority groups and local community relations councils. The Commission financially and otherwise helps activities connected with its aims.

A nationwide survey taken by Opinion Research Centre (ORC) in early 1981 interviewed over a thousand white and just over a thousand ethnic minority people. Just over a half of each group had not even heard of the CRE. Of those who had, about 40% of both groups thought the CRE was doing a good job. About 20% thought it was doing a bad job. While 11% of whites approved of the CRE for "looking after the interests of minorities", 18% of whites thought the CRE was "too biased in favour of minorities". Ethnic minorities who were critical of the CRE felt that racial problems in Britain were getting worse.

Another survey in late 1981 (after the mid-year riots) showed much more support for the Commission. 80% of ethnic minority people and 60% of whites favoured more government support to the Commission for tackling racial discrimination.

The CRE has been criticized from all sides – both for not doing enough and for doing too much. A late 1981 report by an all-party committee of MPs called for the CRE to drastically cut its activities. The committee felt that much of what was being done should come from government departments. MPs felt the CRE should employ more lawyers and concentrate on exposing discrimination more effectively.

# The Media

Many white people rely on the media for the images, information and ideas they have about blacks. This is especially true of whites who do not personally know people from ethnic minorities. A 1981 CRE report on *Public Awareness and the Media* criticized the media for tending to put black people into the news for negative reasons. It was noted that the black population was presented as a "problem" and essentially different from mainstream society. The report urged the media to play a more constructive role in the picture it presented of ethnic minorities.

The National Union of Journalists has produced guidelines for writing about race and reporting about racist organizations. These guidelines include points such as "Only mention someone's race or nationality if it is strictly relevant", "Resist the temptation to sensationalize issues which could harm race relations", and "Seek to achieve wider and better coverage of black affairs:social, political, cultural." There is also an organization called "Campaign Against Racism in the Media" (CARM).

In 1982 the CRE published a report on *Television in a Multi-Racial Society*. This concluded that "the opportunities for and presentation of ethnic minority actors were still very limited and restrictive in both frequency and variety of roles cast . . . . It is doubtful whether the majority of roles portrayed contribute towards racial harmony and integration in our society."

Channel Four began broadcasting in late 1982 with more opportunities for ethnic minority performers. New programmes such as *Ebony*, with black presenters, began to focus on black issues. But the CRE report stresses that multi-racial casting and programmes for and about minorities should be more a part of *all* channels. Ethnic minority actors should have a similar range of opportunities to white actors. Also, writers should be encouraged to write more scripts which reflect the multi-racial nature of British society.

In early 1983 the country's first Asian soap opera began on BBC Radio Leicester for the Asian community in the East Midlands. The programme, called *Kanhani Apni Apni* ("Our Stories"), revolves around the lives and loves of the Patels, a fictional immigrant family. The heroine Leela comes from India to marry her fiance Navin. The actors are all local amateurs. The series is broadcast in English. By looking at the problems Leela faces, the programmes are meant to help real Asians with difficulties they have.

Black and Asian broadcasters are now seen and heard on national as well as local television and radio. BBC local radio stations have a number of ethnic programmes and presenters. One of the oldest programmes especially for Asians is on BBC Radio Leicester. Radio stations in London, Stoke-on-Trent, Derby, Leeds, Nottingham and Oxford also have programmes for Asian listeners.

Asian actress Sneh Gupta became the motel's receptionist in television's *Crossroads* in 1982. This is part of a move to include more ethnic minority performers in Britain's theatres and media.

# Police and Crime

Less than half of 1% of police officers in England and Wales are black. Lord Scarman commented in 1982 that the 1981 inner city riots were not race riots but anti-police riots: "You cannot police a multi-racial society with a police force which does not reflect this ethnic diversity."

The number of people from ethnic groups applying to join the Metropolitan Police in 1982 was more than double the number for 1981. But attracting recruits from ethnic minorities is difficult, especially among West Indians, many of whom see the police as an enemy.

In an opinion poll shown by London Weekend Television in 1982, 44% of the London sample

PC Raymond Campbell (left) and PC Mohinder Mattoo. PC Campbell was born in Jamaica and came to Britain at age eleven. He served nine years in the Royal Marines. He believes it is "five times more difficult" to be a black policeman than a white one. The police are trying to encourage more recruits from ethnic minorities.

thought the average policeman was "unconsciously racially prejudiced". Another 9% thought he was "deliberately racially prejudiced". 33% thought the police "not racially prejudiced at all". (A nationwide *Observer* newspaper poll in 1981 found 30% of the sample thinking the police biased against blacks.)

The Police Training Council has been reviewing training in race relations. Cadets and recruits are encouraged to learn all about the history, culture and lifestyle of racial minorities. In 1982 there was some dispute as to whether police should also be studying racism, and looking at their own attitudes. A local councillor said: "There was no problem while the course simply introduced other people's cultures. But when an anti-racist element was introduced, including an examination of cadets' own attitudes, there were difficulties."

There has been a radical shift in police training since the 1981 riots and the recommendations of the Scarman Report. In the new "Human Awareness Training", many police are now being taught to examine their own behaviour – trying to identify and cope with any prejudices they have.

Brixton (South London), April 1981. Youth and police clash. One black onlooker said: "This has been building up for a long time. This is not against the white community, this is against the police. They treat us like dirt, like second-class citizens." A Community/Police Consultative Group was set up after the riots to bring more openness and trust into police/community relations. Brixton is an area where black youths are three times more likely to remain unemployed than if they were white. The area also has the highest proportion of single-parent families in the country. The media has spotlighted Brixton for its problems – but there are many positive aspects to the area which receive less attention. Many community organizations are working to improve local conditions. Over forty different events featuring local talent entertain at Brixton's yearly Festival.

In early 1983 the Hendon Police Training School opened a language laboratory, believed to be the first of its kind in the world. Police are being trained to understand dialects, including the patois terms being used by London's black communities.

## CRIME

Police in London have been noting "colour" on their records since 1961. In 1982, for the first time, Scotland Yard made public the racial figures in just one area of crime – muggings. The Yard's 1981 records showed that 55% of victims of "street robbery of personal property" said their attackers were coloured. 26% said they were white. The rest either couldn't tell or were attacked by groups of mixed race.

Many people opposed the publication of these figures as misleading and damaging to race

relations. The British Council of Churches said: "This makes life difficult for many black people. They are as opposed to crime and violence as anyone . . . many black people feel they have been branded as criminals." Blacks may (or may not) be disproportionately represented in this area of crime, but muggings are in fact less than 1% of all serious offences reported in London in 1981. A 1981 Home Office report did show that Asians are 50 times and blacks 36 times more likely than whites to be the *victims* of assaults.

## PRISONS

In 1982 ethnic minorities were only about 4% of Britain's population – but occupied nearly 20% of prison places. In some borstals the figures were over 40%. Most of these minority people were Afro-Caribbean.

The disproportionate number of blacks in UK prisons may be due partly to the extra problems minorities face. One senior probation officer has said: "If you gave coloured people opportunities their natural energy and enterprise would achieve a lot. Instead, we sit on them." The National Association for Care and Resettlement of Offenders (NACRO) suggests that there is some discrimination in blacks being more likely than whites to receive prison sentences rather than probation orders or community work scheme orders for similar offences.

There are some racial conflicts in prisons between staff and inmates, and between prisoners themselves. The prison service has been increasingly concerned. There are now Race Relations Officers in every establishment. A 1982 seminar suggested handbooks for staff about racial minorities. The prison service is trying to attract more officers from ethnic minorities (fewer than 1% are from minorities so far).

Conflict between police and West Indian Rastafarians has been especially sharp. Rastafarians are followers of a religion which began in Jamaica in the 1930s. Rastas regard themselves as Africans exiled in Western

countries. Former Emperor Haile Selassie I of Ethiopia is regarded as having been the Black Messiah. Rastas smoke marijuana (which they call *"ganja"*) as a wisdom weed. This is illegal in Britain. Many Rastas who are in prison are there for drug offences. Rastafarian hair is usually kept in long tight braids known as "dreadlocks". In 1982 the prison department became easier on the issue of haircuts for Rastas. A 1976 ruling regarded Rastafarians as a "political" sect among West Indians – but new instructions in 1983 were to treat this more as a "religion".

## RIOTS

Blacks complain that they are more likely than whites to be stopped by police. There are also complaints that ethnic minorities are not treated as well by police. In the early 1980s there were riots in several cities, sparked off by conflict between police officers and young blacks. Since then there have been renewed efforts to improve police relations with minority groups.

There have been racial clashes in Britain before: for example, in Cardiff (1919), Liverpool (1948), Deptford (1949), Camden Town (1954), Nottingham and Notting Hill (1958), Notting Hill Carnival (1976), Southall (1979), Bristol (1980), and Toxteth and Brixton (1981).

The 1981 riots had a strong effect on black community leaders. They came together in a new way. As one leader said: "We realized we didn't know the system. Toxteth and Brixton brought it home to people that something had to be done."

Black Rights UK was launched in 1982 at a meeting in London. There were representatives of the judiciary, the churches, police and two hundred delegates from community groups. As a charity, the initiative provides advice and representation, and financial help encouraging ethnic minorities to qualify as lawyers. The non-charitable side lobbies for social changes to help ethnic groups.

# Politics

An organization began in 1982 called the Consortium of Ethnic Minority Groups. Its sole purpose is to have black candidates selected for winnable Parliamentary seats. There have been no black MPs in Britain since the 1920s. There have been, however, two West Indian members of the House of Lords (Lord Constantine and Lord Pitt) and Lord Chitnis, an Asian.

Ethnic minorities are showing increasing interest in the political system. For the 1974 General Elections only 63% of Afro-Caribbeans and 73% of Asians had registered to vote. This had increased to 81% and 77% for the 1979 election, compared to about 93% for the general population. The ethnic minority vote can be especially important because the minorities are so concentrated in several city areas.

A 1980 survey found that ethnic minorities rate various issues somewhat differently from the general population. On a list of fourteen election items, ethnic minorities rated "improving race relations" 7th in importance. Whites put this much further down the list, at 12th.

Russell Profitt came to Britain at the age of thirteen from Guyana. He has been a deputy headmaster and a local councillor. He is one of a number of ethnic minority leaders hoping to become an MP and was a candidate in 1979. There were seventeen Afro-Caribbean and Asian candidates standing for Parliament in the 1983 election – but none were elected. The last black MP was in the 1920s – an Indian in the constituency of Battersea North. There were also two Indian MPs elected to Parliament in the nineteenth century.

# Sport

There has been a growing involvement of ethnic minorities (especially West Indians) in British cricket, boxing, athletics, and, more recently, football. West Indians coming to Britain in the 1950s and 1960s knew cricket but had little interest in soccer. The children of these immigrants, however, have taken to football. There is also considerable black involvement in such sports as tennis, table tennis, karate, wrestling, weight-lifting, judo, squash, netball, rounders – and dominoes. Dominoes has become a popular West Indian pastime, with many leagues and clubs and tournaments. Games are usually played as part of a social outing involving coachloads of players and their families.

Laurie Cunningham was Britain's first £1 million black football player. By 1982 there were 27 black footballers playing regularly in the top two divisions of the English League – and more in lower divisions.

# Arts and Celebrations

Britain's ethnic minorities display rich talent in music, dance, drama, painting, literature .... In some places this is appreciated and is being encouraged. All too often, however, ethnic arts are, as the title of a publication describes them, "the arts Britain ignores". The Commission for Racial Equality has been urging more support for ethnic minority arts.

In 1976 an organization called MAAS – Minorities Arts Advisory Service – was formed. This helps to link, publicize and advise local

"Aswad", a leading UK reggae band. Reggae is a style of black music which originated in Kingston, Jamaica. West Indian music has become very popular in Britain since the 1960s.

groups and centres, many of which are struggling to survive. The Rainbow Art Group was organized in 1978 to promote the work of visual artists from ethnic minorities.

There are many local ethnic arts activities. These include such groups as Drum Arts Centre and the Black Theatre of Brixton, both in London, and Inkworks in Bristol. Many ethnic community centres are also involved with the arts, such as the Liverpool Merseyside Caribbean Centre near to a Pakistani cultural centre, and the Bengali Kobi Nazrul Centre in London's East End. Aklowa Dancers and Drummers was formed in 1977 to perform

dances, songs and drumming from West Africa.

Among the Cypriot community there is a Cypriot Community Centre in northwest London. This teaches English and Greek language and also Greek dance. The Greek-Cypriot Theatro Technis was formed in 1957. The plays performed deal with themes important to Greek-Cypriots here.

Sometimes English performers are brought in as well. A Chinese tractor mechanic from Liverpool worked out a form of mime drama using both English and Chinese actors. The first play was shown both in Liverpool and at London's Royal Court Theatre.

Omnibus was set up as a West Indian theatre group in Notting Hill. Carib Theatre Productions is a small touring theatre specializing in plays from the West Indies. Mustapha Matura is among the most celebrated UK-based West Indian playwrights. (The *Evening Standard* voted him "most promising playwright of the year 1974").

Folk dances known as Raas and Garba are very popular among the Gujarati Indian population. These dances involve both men and women, clapping pairs of sticks. Leicester's annual Raas and Garba festival began in 1971. This attracts teams of dancers from all over the Midlands.

A popular folk dance among Punjabis is *"bhangra"*, which is a fiery harvest dance. Over a dozen amateur groups in Britain put on performances. The prize-winning Punjab Bhangra Group of Wolverhampton has been run by a Punjabi policeman. He came to Britain at the age of twelve, speaking no English, and was one of the first Asians to become a British police cadet.

The first UK Asian Song Contest took place in 1975. Young Asian music is very much a mixture of eastern and western cultures. The Indian instrument called a *"tabla"* may be used for percussion along with western instruments such as guitars. The group look is very trendy western. At the first song contest, finalists were chosen from heats in Southall, Bedford, Leicester, Manchester, Leeds and Birmingham.

The first Asian Youth Festival also took place in 1975, with performers from all over the country.

Several young Asian pop singers in Britain have made hit records. Nazia Hassan is a young London Pakistani girl whose record "Disco Deewane" (Disco Crazy) has been popular in the cities of South Asia as well as in Britain.

There are also classical Indian music and dance performers in the UK. The Centre for Indian Arts has promoted an annual Indian Arts Festival at the South Bank in London since 1970.

Films from Hong Kong are a favourite entertainment for the Chinese in Britain. There are often special showings in Chinese areas at 1 am for restaurant workers. Many films are also imported from India. (The Indian film industry produces more films than any other country in the world.) By the mid-1970s there were over forty full-time Asian cinemas in Britain. Many ordinary cinemas organized regular Asian film sessions on Sunday mornings. Since the video boom of the early 1980s, many Asians now watch imported films in their own homes.

Asian cinemas are used also for other cultural events and performances. Amongst Pakistanis and Muslim Indians in Britain *"Mushairas"* are very popular. These are poetry evenings, with poets reciting their work in person. *Mushairas* are held about four times a year in Birmingham and other cities with large Pakistani populations – Bradford, London, Manchester, Glasgow and Leeds.

## CELEBRATIONS

Britain's New Commonwealth and Pakistani ethnic minorities celebrate a number of holidays and festivals, some of which are linked to religion. The exact dates often vary from year to year. Here is a description of just a few of these on the dates they occurred in 1982-83:

● August Bank Holiday: *Notting Hill Carnival:* This yearly carnival began in 1965 as a local event and has grown to attract many thousands of people from all over Britain.

Three British politicians try their hand at West Indian steel drums. This was part of an all-party rally against racism held in Trafalgar Square in the late 1970s. (Steel drums began in the West Indies after World War II. Oil drums and other scrap from junkyards were used to make music. The drum has developed from this into a proper instrument which can be finely tuned. A whole range of notes are possible. Steel bands are popular in schools and youth clubs in several areas – over 20 in London alone.)

Dazzling costumes and steel bands are a feature enlivening the streets. "Carnival" (called "maas" in the Caribbean) is a tradition of Trinidad. A somewhat smaller yearly carnival was started in Leeds in 1968.

● September: *Miss Afro-Westindian Beauty Pageant:* First held in 1975, this is a yearly competition "to achieve greater recognition for black beauty".

● 16-27 October 1982: *Dussehra/Dashara:* This is one of the most popular and widely celebrated Hindu festivals. There are processions and dancing, family reunions and the exchange of gifts. In India the celebrations extend over ten days, but Asians in Britain often shorten this to four or five days.

● I November 1982: *Birthday of Guru Nanak (1469-1539):* Guru Nanak was the founder of the Sikh religion and his birthday is the

◀Indrapriya David, a Sri Lankan teacher at the Commonwealth Institute in London, performed an Indian classical dance in Trafalgar Square. (There are over 45,000 Sri Lankans living and working in the UK.)

holiest festival of the Sikhs. There are hymns, speeches and talks about his life and teachings throughout the day.

- 15 November 1982: *Diwali:* Lamps are lit, house fronts illuminated and presents are exchanged for this Hindu New Year Festival of Lights. Lakshmi, the goddess of prosperity, is supposed to visit houses lit by many lamps.

- 13 February 1983: *Yuan Tan:* The Chinese New Year is the most important festival in the Chinese calendar. It is a time for visiting friends and family, clearing debts and buying new clothes. Presents are exchanged and children are given lucky money in red envelopes. Everyone wishes each other prosperity with the words *"Kung Hei Fat Choy"*. Festivals include street celebrations, especially the Lion Dances in Soho, London. This is the time when the Kitchen God ascends to heaven to report on each member of the family.

- 27 February 1983: *Teng Chieh:* The Lantern Festival officially marks the end of the Chinese New Year and the re-opening of public offices. Lanterns appear on market stalls and decorate homes, restaurants and temples. Fireworks are exploded. The high spot of the festival is the parade or dance of the dragon. The dragon is usually over 100 feet long and made from a frame of bamboo covered with brightly coloured and embroidered silk or paper. It is carried by men through the streets. Money wrapped in red paper is hung from upstairs windows as an offering or gift for the dragon.

- March 1983: *Holi:* Bonfires, street dancing, and processions give colour to this five-day Hindu spring festival.

- 12 June 1983: Start of *Ramadan:* This is a month of fasting from sunrise to sunset. The fast celebrates the sending down of the Qur'an (Koran) as a holy guide for mankind. Muslims fast as a way of experiencing self-discipline. The dates of Ramadan are about ten days earlier with each new year.

- 11 July 1983: *Eid-Ul-Fitr:* This Festival of Fast Breaking celebrates the end of the fasting month of Ramadan. Charity is given to the poor. Money and new clothes are given to children. Cards are sent to distant friends.

Leeds Carnival began in 1968 and now takes place every August. By 1975 it was attracting four steel bands and nearly five hundred costumed "maas" dancers.

"Yuan Tan", the Chinese New Year, celebrated in Soho, London. It was in the 1950s that London's "Chinatown" moved from the East End to Gerrard Street, Soho. (The local Chinatown in Liverpool has been around Nelson Street for over fifty years.) 1983 was the "Year of the Pig". 1984, the "Year of the Rat", started again the twelve-year cycle. There are characteristics surrounding each year – supposedly affecting the personalities of people as they are born.

# Resources List

## Sourcebooks for teachers:
MINORITIES: A TEACHER'S RESOURCE BOOK FOR THE MULTIETHNIC CURRICULUM by David Hicks (1981, Heinemann Educational Books).
RESOURCES FOR MULTI-CULTURAL EDUCATION: AN INTRODUCTION by Gillian Klein (1982, Longman Resources Unit, 33-35 Tanner Row, York). This includes a list of local centres throughout the country concerned with multicultural education, that offer in-service courses and collections of materials.
THE DEVELOPMENT PUZZLE by Nance Fyson (1984, CWDE/Hodder & Stoughton Educational). Background information on development issues in Third World countries, ideas for teaching, and full section of resources available. Titles relating to "India", "The Caribbean", etc, can be found in the topic and subject listings.
ACER RESOURCE AND INFORMATION GUIDE (1983, The Afro-Caribbean Education Resource Project). Booklet listing organizations and resource centres, reports and documents, audio-visual aids, journals. (See ACER address in list of organizations.)

## Some sources of booklists:
CENTRE FOR URBAN EDUCATIONAL STUDIES (CUES), Robert Montifiore Building, Underwood Rd, London E1 5AD (Tel: 01-377 0040).
The CUES library has a collection of pupil information books and fiction relevant to cultural diversity. CUES publications include
- Assessing children's books for the multi-ethnic society (free sheet)
- The multi-cultural society: background reading for teachers and librarians (free list)
- The multi-cultural society: bookshops, including those set up by ethnic minorities
- The multi-cultural society: useful addresses
- Fiction for secondary schools

COMMONWEALTH INSTITUTE Library and Resource Centre, Kensington High Street, London W8 6NQ (Tel: 01-602 3252).
- An annotated series of basic bibliographies on Commonwealth countries and topics, with publication details. Periodicals included
- Checklists on Commonwealth literature; Checklist on African literature; Checklist on Caribbean literature; Checklist on Indian literature

NATIONAL BOOK LEAGUE, Book House, 45 East Hill, London SW18 2QZ (Tel: 01-870 9055).
Several booklists especially relevant are:
- "We All Live Here", 1983 multi-cultural booklist. Over 100 titles
- Stories and settings booklist includes "Africa", "The Americas" and "Asia and Australasia"

## Some books:
BRITAIN'S BLACK POPULATION (1980, Heinemann Educational Books). Education, housing, employment and health examined in terms of official policy and statistics.
OUR LIVES: YOUNG PEOPLE'S AUTO-BIOGRAPHIES (1979, ILEA English Centre). Anthology of accounts by young people of various nationalities of their own experiences, including immigration to Britain.
IMMIGRANTS AND MINORITIES IN BRITISH SOCIETY (1978, Allen & Unwin). Overview of migration and settlement in the UK.
Open University Course E354 on ETHNIC MINORITIES AND COMMUNITY RELATIONS Ten units published (1982, Open University Educational Enterprises Ltd).
RACE IN BRITAIN – CONTINUITY AND CHANGE (1982, Hutchinson). Overview and background to minorities.
(see also COMMISSION FOR RACIAL EQUALITY books and booklets)

## Some bookshops:
SOMA BOOKS (INDEPENDENT PUBLISHING), 38 Kennington Lane, London SE11 (Tel: 01-735 2101).
Books on and from the Indian subcontinent for children and adults, in English and main Asian languages. Some Afro-Caribbean as well.
WALTER RODNEY BOOKSHOP (BOGLE L'OUVERTURE PUBLICATIONS), 5a Chignell Place, London W13 (Tel: 01-579 4920).
Afro-Caribbean books and race relations. Includes novels for juniors and secondary.

## Some sources of visual aids:
CONCORD FILMS COUNCIL LTD, 201 Felixstowe Rd, Ipswich, Suffolk IP3 9BJ (Tel: 0473 76012 & 715754).
Library of films and videos for hire, including many relevant to race relations in Britain. Some of the titles available in the catalogue include: "Asians in Britain"; "A Mosque in the Park"; "Multi-cultural Education"; "Multi-racial Britain Series (10)"; "Race and the Inner City"; "Schools and Race".
"TUIREG", TRADE UNION INTERNATIONAL RESEARCH & EDUCATION GROUP, Ruskin College, Walton St, Oxford OX1 2HE (Tel: 0865 54599).
"They Think They Are English". Tape/slide programme (15 min). Deals with common myths about immigrants, especially related to employment. Shows how immigrants were urged to come to Britain, doing jobs British unwilling to do. Family from India gives point of view. Sale or hire.
HELP THE AGED EDUCATION DEPT. 318, St.Paul's Rd, London N1 (Tel: 01-359 6316).
"Growing Old – An Indian Experience". 32 colour slides and notes about the old in a village in southern India. "Growing Old – The Jamaican Experience". 32 slides and notes about elderly Jamaicans now living in Britain, as well as the old in rural Jamaica.
FILM FORUM, 56 Brewer St, London W1 (Tel: 01-437 6487).
"Our People", Series of six films, 25 min each, produced by Thames Television, on race relations and history of immigration in Britain. Hire.

## Some periodicals:
MULTICULTURAL TEACHING (three issues a year), 30 Wenger Crescent, Trentham, Stoke-on-Trent, ST4 8LE.
Practical approaches, resources, events, for teachers.
RACE TODAY (monthly), Towards Racial Justice, 184 Kings Cross Rd, London WC1.
Campaigning, from a black perspective.
(see also COMMISSION FOR RACIAL EQUALITY and NATIONAL ASSOCIATION FOR MULTIRACIAL EDUCATION – NAME listings)

## Some organizations and associations:
AFRO-CARIBBEAN EDUCATION RESEARCH PROJECT (ACER), 275 Kennington Lane, London SE11 (Tel: 01-582 2771).
Collects and collates Afro-Caribbean and British Afro-Caribbean materials suitable for education; has developed own materials. Small reference library on the Caribbean.
CARIBBEAN TEACHERS' ASSOCIATION, 8 Camberwell Green, London SE5 (Tel: 01-708 1293).
Works on behalf of teachers, mainly of Caribbean origin, to promote a more multicultural curriculum in schools.
CENTRE FOR MULTICULTURAL EDUCATION, University of London Institute of Education, Bedford Way, London WC1 (Tel: 01-636 1500).
Conferences, provides speakers, assists teachers and colleges of education, and supports research.
CENTRE FOR WORLD DEVELOPMENT EDUCATION, 128 Buckingham Palace Rd, London SW1 (Tel: 01-730 8332/3).
Promotes education in Britain about development issues and Britain's interdependence with the Third World. Catalogue of

materials, mail-order, resources centre. Many of materials are about countries of origin of immigrants to UK. For example: "Village Industries", slide sets and photo set on village industries in India; "Caribbean in Change", slide sets about rural and urban life, tourism, sugar production, and Caribbean links with the EEC.

COMMISSION FOR RACIAL EQUALITY, Elliott House, 10/12 Allington St, London SW1 (Tel: 01-828 7022).
Set up to support Race Relations Act of 1976, investigate discrimination, promote racial harmony. Publications, some free. Library open to public. Journals include "New Equals" (bi-monthly) and "New Community" (two issues a year). Lists of ethnic minority press and ethnic minority organizations available, also local Community Relations Councils throughout Britain.

COMMONWEALTH INSTITUTE, Kensington High Street, London W8 (Tel: 01-603 4535).
Displays, exhibitions, performances relating to Commonwealth countries. Bookshop, extensive library, loan of audio-visual materials, eg music from Africa, the Caribbean, India. Publications, including fact booklets on many countries.

COMMONWEALTH INSTITUTE, SCOTLAND, 8 Rutland Sq, Edinburgh (Tel: 031-229 6668).
Resource material; library facilities on books and filmstrips, reference library.

COMMUNITY AND RACE RELATIONS UNIT OF THE BRITISH COUNCIL OF CHURCHES (CRRU), 2 Eaton Gate, London SW1W 9BL (Tel: 01-730 9611).
Resource centre; Publications include "Resources for a plural society" and a "National Front pack" of study documents.

EAST LONDON EDUCATION RESOURCE CENTRE, Centre for Education in a Multi-ethnic Society, Robert Montifiore Building, Underwood Rd, London E1 5AD (Tel: 01-377 9934).
English and Asian language resources on the Indian subcontinent for teachers and pupils.

INSTITUTE OF RACE RELATIONS (IRR), 247 Pentonville Rd, London N1 (Tel: 01-837 0041).
Educational body working with black and anti-racist groups. Library of books and journals on race and minority relations. Some publications.

MINORITY ARTS ADVISORY SERVICE (MAAS), Beauchamp Lodge, 2 Warwick Crescent, London W2 (Tel: 01-286 1854).
Publishes an annual register of ethnic minority performers, many of whom are willing to perform in schools.

MULTICULTURAL EDUCATION UNIT, BRADFORD COLLEGE, Great Horton Rd, Bradford, West Yorkshire, BD7 1AY (Tel: 0274 34844).
Contributes to in-service training, links with related organizations in UK, resource information bank.

NATIONAL ASSOCIATION FOR MULTIRACIAL EDUCATION (NAME), 86 Station Rd, Mickleover, Derby DE3 22FP.
National pressure group, annual conference; concerned with issues of language, anti-racist teaching, etc. Members are mainly teachers. Termly journal: "Multiracial education". Central address can supply addresses of local NAME groups. London NAME, 43 Anson Rd, N7, has loan exhibitions and publishes its own termly journal, "Issues".

NATIONAL COUNCIL FOR MOTHER TONGUE TEACHING (NCMTT), 5 Musgrave Crescent, London SW6 4PT (Tel: 01-736 2134)
Promotes the education of children growing up in a two-language environment. Conferences, exhibitions, workshops, publications.

RUNNYMEDE TRUST, 37A Grays Inn Rd, London WC1 (Tel: 01-405 7703).
Research and education on all aspects of race relations. Publications. Monthly "Runnymede Trust Bulletin" provides comprehensive summary of current events relating to immigrants and ethnic minorities.

**Some local centres:**
The following centres are provided by local education authorities. These centres supply information about locally available materials related to multicultural education and the backgrounds of ethnic minorities.

AVON Multicultural Education Centre, Bishop Rd, Bishopston, Bristol BS7 8LS

BEDFORD Resources Centre, Acacia Rd, Bedford MK42 0HU

BIRMINGHAM Language Centre, The Bordesley Centre, Camp Hill, Stratford Rd, Birmingham B11 1AR

BLACKBURN Language Centre, Accrington Rd, Blackburn, Lancashire BB1 2AS

BRADFORD T.F. Davies Centre for Teachers, Rosemount, Clifton Villas, Manningham Lane, Bradford BD8 7BY

BRENT Multicultural Resources Centre, Brent Teachers' Centre, Ealing Rd, Alperton, Wembley, Middx HA0 4QL

BURNLEY Language Centre, Stoneyholme School, Burleigh Street, Burnley, Lancashire

COVENTRY Minority Group Support Service, Community Education Centre, Southfields, South Street, Coventry CV1 5EJ

DERBY Resources Centre, Madeley Centre, Rosehill Street, Derby DE3 1GT

EALING Ealing Teachers' Centre, Ealing (Northern) Sports Centre, Greenford Rd, Greenford, Middx UB6 0HU

ENFIELD English Language Centre, Tile Kiln Lane, London N13 8RY

GLASGOW Language Teaching Centre, 39 Napiershall Street, Glasgow G20

HALIFAX Immigrant Teaching Service, West House, King Cross Street, Halifax, West Yorks HX1 1EB

HARINGEY Multicultural Curriculum Support Group, St Mary's C of E Junior School, Rectory Gardens, London N8

HARROW Multicultural Support Group, Little Stanmore School, Camrose Ave, Harrow HA8 65A

HOUNSLOW Schools Language Unit, The Old Isleworth and Science School, London Rd, Isleworth, Middx TW3 4DN

KIRKLEES Reading and Language Centre, Hopton, Mirfield, West Yorks WR14 8PR

LEEDS John Taylor Teachers' Centre, 53 Headingly Lane, Leeds LS6 1AA

LEICESTER Rushymead Language Centre, Harrison Rd, Leicester LE4 7PA

LIVERPOOL Crown Street Language Centre, 7 Crown Street, Liverpool L7 3PA

LUTON MERC, Tennyson Rd Primary School, Luton, Bedfordshire LU1 3RS

MANCHESTER Multicultural Development Service, The Anson Rd Centre, 11 Anson Rd, Manchester M14 5BY

MIDDLESBOROUGH Centre for Multicultural Education, c/o Victoria Rd Primary School, Victoria Rd, Cleveland TS1 3QF

NEWHAM Centre for English as a Second Language, New City Road School, New City Rd, London E13 9PY

NORTHAMPTON Multiracial Education Centre, Teachers' Centre, Barry Rd, Northampton NN1 5JS

NOTTINGHAM Language Centre, Goldswong Terrace, Cranmer St, Nottingham NG3 4HA

OLDHAM The Greengate Centre, Greengate St, Oldham, Lancs OL4 1RY

OXFORD Centre for Multicultural Education, Oxford First School, Union St, Oxford OX4 1JP

PETERBOROUGH Centre for Multiracial Education, 165a Cromwell Rd, Peterborough PE1 2EL

READING The Language Centre, Lydford Rd, Reading, Berkshire RG1 5OH

SANDWELL Ethnic Minority Support Service, Churchbridge Teachers' Centre, Churchbridge, Oldbury, Warley, West Midlands B69 2AX

SLOUGH Co-ordinator for Multicultural Education, Thomas Gray Language Centre, Queens Rd, Slough, Berkshire SL1 3OW

SOUTHAMPTON ESL Resource Base, Mountpleasant Middle School, Mountpleasant Rd, Southampton, Hampshire SO9 3TQ

WALSALL Walsall Language Service, Educational Development Centre, 36 Wolverhampton Rd, Walsall WS2 HPN

WALTHAM FOREST Waltham Forest Teachers' Centre, Queen's Rd, Walthamstow, London E17 8QS

WOLVERHAMPTON Multicultural Resources Centre, Beckminster House, Birches Barn Rd, Wolverhampton WV3 7BJ

# Index

Figures in **bold type** refer to page numbers of illustrations and captions